Pioneers of Modern Spirituality

Pioneers of Modern Spirituality

The Neglected Anglican Innovators
of a 'Spiritual but not Religious' Age

Jane Shaw

CHURCH
PUBLISHING
INCORPORATED

First published in Great Britain in 2018 by
Darton, Longman and Todd Ltd
1 Spencer Court
140–142 Wandsworth High Street
London SW18 4JJ

First published in the United States in 2018 by
Church Publishing
19 East 34th Street
New York, NY 10016
www.churchpublishing.org

Cover design by Jennifer Kopec, 2Pug Design
Typeset by Kerrypress, St. Albans

A record of this book is available from the Library of Congress.

ISBN-13: 978-0-89869-167-2 (pbk.)
ISBN-13: 978-0-89869-170-2 (ebook)

Printed in the United States of America

For the monks of the Society of St John the Evangelist
in Massachusetts

Brothers, friends, spiritual mentors

Contents

Acknowledgments

This book began as the Sarum Lectures, which I delivered in April and May 2017, and I am very grateful to the Principal of Sarum College, James Woodward, and the then Dean of Salisbury, June Osborne (now Bishop of Llandaff) for their kind invitation and very generous hospitality. It was a great pleasure to deliver the lectures in Salisbury Cathedral to a warm and encouraging audience, and I thank all those who attended so faithfully over four evenings and also contributed so much to the Question and Answer periods following the lectures and to a final fifth session in which we discussed the import of these figures and their work for Christian life and the Anglican Church today. I also thank Christine Nielson-Craig, and all the staff of Sarum College and its bookstore, who offered help and a warm welcome, along with the canons of Salisbury Cathedral, especially Robert Titley and the former Precentor Jeremy Davies.

Several friends have offered ideas, commentary and encouragement along the way, especially Sarah Ogilvie and Rebecca Lyman who read a draft of this book, Vincent Strudwick who read drafts of the lectures, and Linda Woodhead who discussed the initial framing of the lectures with me, and I thank them. I am grateful to the late Bob Jeffery for a conversation about Reginald Somerset Ward, and to Peter Francis, Warden of Gladstone's Library, for his gracious hospitality in offering me several days in that marvelous library when I was working out how to turn the lectures into a book. I thank, also, the librarians at Lambeth Palace Library where

I worked on Reginald Somerset Ward's papers, and at Trinity College, Cambridge, where I read the Rose Macaulay archive.

This book is dedicated to the monks of the Society of St John the Evangelist in Massachusetts, the order to which Father Johnson, in Chapter 4, belonged. For more than thirty years, they have offered me spiritual support, encouragement and solace, and a place of rest in busy times, both at their monastery in Cambridge, Massachusetts, and at Emery House, their retreat house in the country, near Boston. In particular, Curtis Almquist has offered his characteristically abundant hospitality, spiritual wisdom and counsel on numerous occasions. In several ways, the themes of this book have flowed out of time spent with these brothers. Many years ago, at Emery House, I picked up the first volume of Rose Macaulay's letters to Father Johnson, and couldn't put it down. Kind invitations from Geoffrey Tristram, then Superior, to preach at the monastery's 2014 Fellowship day, and in 2015 to lead the annual summer retreat for all the monks, offered me wonderful opportunities to begin thinking through some of the ideas here. James Koester, the current Superior, has been a fund of knowledge and engaging conversation about Father Johnson, and he also very kindly retrieved Father Johnson's papers from storage for me and gave me permission to read them. Father David Allen, who knew Father Johnson, has offered me his memories of that monk who was Rose Macaulay's friend. It is appropriate that I finished writing this book when once again in the company of the SSJE brothers, at Emery House.

Thanks to the teams at Darton, Longman and Todd in the UK, especially David Moloney, and Church Publishing in the USA, especially Nancy Bryan.

Introduction

'Church going has declined steadily and rapidly; this being a free and honest age, people no longer attend what they do not like.' So declared the Anglican priest Percy Dearmer in a set of lectures he delivered in New York (and later London) in 1919. He went on to suggest how the situation had changed. 'Fifty years ago, men like Charles Dickens went regularly to church; … they grumbled, but still they went. To-day they do not even grumble.'[1]

This book is about four people, all Anglican, two women and two men, from the early twentieth century, who were engaged in and influenced by a revival of spirituality: the writer and spiritual director Evelyn Underhill; the priest and spiritual director Reginald Somerset Ward; the priest and scholar Percy Dearmer; and the novelist Rose Macaulay, who shares her chapter with the priest and monk Hamilton Johnson SSJE, the person who gently guided her back to faith when she was 69 years old. Each of them is worth a fresh look in their own right. Each has something to teach us about prayer, worship, and how we cultivate a relationship with God. Each was something of a pioneer, but has been somewhat neglected in recent years.

But there are further reasons for looking at them: they were all committed to the revival of spirituality at a moment when people were questioning institutional religion more than ever before. The usual expression of Christian faith – going to church – began to decline, both as a habit of spiritual being and a societal expectation, but this did not mean people were no longer searching and questing after some form of ultimate meaning. Faith was being revitalized in other ways: through the cultivation of an individual prayer life, in retreats and a great flourishing of interest in mysticism, and through the arts. All four major figures in this book, at some time or another, sat at the edges of the church, or even outside it, and called it to an engagement with the world and a rediscovery of the depths of its own tradition. This gives their work – a century ago - a resonance in our own 'spiritual but not religious' age.

The observations that Dearmer made in 1919 were reiterated by Evelyn Underhill two years later in her Upton Lectures at Manchester College in Oxford, the topic of which was *The Life of the Spirit and the Life of Today* (the title of her book, published in 1921), and considered the vexed relationship between institutional religion and an individual's spiritual life. She wrote: 'I think we may now say without exaggeration that the general modern judgment – not, of course, the clerical or orthodox judgment – is adverse to institutionalism; at least as it now exists.'[2]

Dearmer and Underhill were reading the signs of their times correctly. The early twentieth century did see the beginning of a decline in institutional religion. Historians have generally come to agree that the first decade of the twentieth century saw about a quarter of the British population going to church on any given Sunday (and it was mostly church – the numbers of those belonging to other religions was very small) and the majority of those churchgoers were women. After that first decade of the century, and in particular after World War I, no significant church growth occurred. In other words, from the 1920s until the present, Britain has seen a waning of *public* religious practice.[3]

The intellectual challenges (from science and biblical criticism) to faith, which undermined for many the churches' credibility on doctrinal grounds, and a broader questioning of institutional legitimacy, especially in the wake of World War I, led to this distancing from – and often disillusionment with – institutional religion. However, numerical decline in church attendance did not mean a lessening of spiritual longing.

What marks out the figures in this book is their recognition of the search for spirituality in that void, *and* their acknowledgment of why institutional religion was not necessarily appealing to people. This makes them interesting figures for our time. Yes, their presumptions about many things were very much of their age, but their questions have surprising echoes with our own preoccupations a hundred years later, as we shall see.

Notes

1 Percy Dearmer, *The Art of Public Worship* (London and Oxford: A.R. Mowbray and Co., 1919)

2 Evelyn Underhill, *The Life of the Spirit and the Life of Today* (New York: E.P. Dutton, 1922), p. 156

3 Clive Field, "'The faith society'? Quantifying religious belonging in Edwardian Britain, 1901-1914', *Journal of Religious History*, Vol. 37, No. 1, March 2013, pp. 39-63.

Chapter 1

Evelyn Underhill
Seeking

Evelyn Underhill was a seeker for much of her life. The early twentieth century was a moment when the seeker emerged as a significant figure, inside, outside and on the margins of the churches, questing after an authentic spirituality. Those familiar with Underhill's work may think of her primarily as a devout Anglican, leader of retreats, Christian writer and a prominent laywoman, called upon to serve on multiple church committees. However, only in 1921 when she was in her mid-forties, did she embrace Anglicanism fully, so it was only in the last two decades of her life, in the 1920s and 30s, before she died aged 65 in 1941, that she was the devout and fully-committed Anglican that we remember.

A decade before Underhill made her definitive turn to the Church of England, her lengthy book, *Mysticism*, was published (1911). Through that publication and a series of shorter books that followed, Underhill brought mysticism to a broad audience in the early part of the twentieth century. Her work was part of a broad revival of interest in mysticism in the early twentieth century, kick-started by W. R. Inge's

Bampton Lectures in Oxford in 1899, published that year as *Christian Mysticism*.[1] Underhill's distinctive contribution to this revival was her suggestion that mysticism was practical and could be learnt by anyone. Through her publications and her work as a spiritual director, she guided many people towards a life of prayer, and through the leading of many retreats she was at the forefront of a rapid growth in retreat-taking in the first half of the twentieth century.

The revival of interest in mysticism relates to the ways in which spirituality began to flourish in these years of the early twentieth century, just as institutional religion began to decline. Religion's traditional authority was shaken by science and historical biblical criticism, especially after the 1860s (Darwin's *Origin of Species* was published in 1859). In that context, W. R. Inge turned to mysticism because he asked: on what authority might faith now rest? It was no longer 'the old seats of authority, the infallible Church and the infallible book' which had been fiercely assailed. Rather the seat of authority was now 'a life or experience.'[2] Mysticism was appealing because it apparently transcended religious institutions and sacred texts; as Inge put it: 'For what has mysticism to do with past and future, with history and prophecy? It is a vision of timeless reality, which is neither born nor dies, being raised above the changes and chances of this mortal life.'[3]

Underhill's Search

It was in that context of questioning that Underhill's own spiritual search occurred. Born in 1875, Underhill was brought up in a well-to-do middle-class family (her father was a barrister) that was nominally Anglican, but which paid little attention to faith. She was educated at home, and briefly at a girls' school in Folkstone (where she was confirmed Anglican), before going to King's College, London, to study first botany and then history and philosophy. She was a deeply practical person, being a good book binder, for example, and she was also an expert sailor, a passion she shared with her husband, whom she had known since childhood as a family friend. She was also artistic, and quite early on she began writing: short stories (published in the *Horlicks Magazine*), poetry, and novels that explored the metaphysical and supernatural - in ways that Charles Williams would later in his novels.

She loved to travel and it was when visiting Italy and many of its churches for the first time in 1898 that a spiritual longing began to stir in her. When she was 29, in 1904, she had a spiritual awakening – a religious experience – but did not formally return to the church for another seventeen years. She was, for a brief while, a member of the esoteric occult group, the Order of the Golden Dawn, and it was through her exploration of Christian hermeticism, which she studied in that group, that she came to the Christian mystical tradition. Her search took her to Roman Catholicism and her intellect took her to the modernist end of Roman Catholicism. She got to the point of almost converting to Roman Catholicism, but two things happened that stopped her. First, she told her husband-to-be, Hubert, and he was appalled – not least because he feared the intimate details of their marriage would be shared in the confessional with a celibate, Roman Catholic priest. Secondly, her thoughts of becoming a Roman Catholic occurred at just the moment that modernists like the priest

George Tyrell were excommunicated, and her conscience would not allow her to go further. As she wrote to a friend in 1911, the year that *Mysticism* was published, 'being myself Modernist on many points, I can't quite get in without suppressions or evasions to which I can't quite bring myself. But I can't accept Anglicanism instead: it seems an integrally different thing. So here I am, going to Mass, and so on of course, but entirely deprived of sacraments.'[4] She remained on the margins of the churches for another decade. This means that when she wrote her big book *Mysticism* and began to take on her own spiritual directees, she was still an outsider, questing and seeking.

Mysticism is a book that draws deeply on a wide range of scholarship and texts, contemporary psychological literature on the subject of religious experience, as well as the Christian mystical tradition – with a particular focus on the medieval mystics of the West. But what was mysticism for Underhill? She was a learned woman, but, in the end, mysticism was for her primarily about love. 'In mysticism that love of truth which we saw as the beginning of all philosophy leaves the merely intellectual sphere and takes on the assured aspect of a personal passion.' Mysticism was for her the essence of religion, and in her book *Mysticism* she defined it as 'the expression of the innate tendency of the human spirit towards complete harmony with the transcendental order.'[5] In an essay written much later, in 1936, she used more distinctly Christian, theological language, and defined mysticism as 'the passionate longing of the soul for God, the unseen Reality, loved, sought, and adored in Himself for Himself alone.' She quoted here the Roman Catholic layman, who by that time had influenced her so much, Baron von Hügel, who described this longing as a 'metaphysical thirst'. And so, she said, 'A mystic is not a person who practices unusual forms of prayer, but a person who is ruled by this thirst. He feels and responds to the overwhelming attraction of God, is sensitive to that attraction; perhaps a little in the same way as the artist is sensitive to the mysterious attraction of visible beauty, and the musician to the mysterious attraction of harmonized sound.' She quoted Augustine's great saying – 'Thou hast made us for thyself, and our hearts shall find no rest save in thee' – as the best explanation for this thirst and thus the appeal of the path of mysticism.

Underhill always wanted to make mysticism available to anybody and everybody who had that thirst, and especially to provide a *practical* form of mysticism for others who were, like her, on a spiritual quest. She wanted to train them how, through 'that loving and devoted attention which we call contemplation,' they could come 'to know a spiritual reality to which we are [otherwise] deaf and blind.' She therefore focused on *practice*: the mystic way, a path of prayer, contemplation and action rooted in love, which anyone could learn. Indeed, she believed that mysticism was really 'the science of the love of God'. It is through that love that we come to knowledge of God – neither emotion nor pure intellect, but love.[6]

After the success of *Mysticism*, she wrote two much shorter books for seekers like herself, *The Mystic Way* in 1913 and *Practical Mysticism* in 1914. The latter attempted to show that mysticism was not an esoteric pastime for the few, but something that was open to all. 'It is to a practical mysticism that the practical man is here invited: to a training of his latent faculties, a bracing and brightening of his languid consciousness, an emancipation from the fetters of appearance, a turning of his attention to new levels of the world.' This was possible for anyone: 'mystical perception – this "ordinary contemplation" as specialists call it – is … a natural human activity, no more involving the great powers and sublime experiences of the mystical saints and philosophers than the ordinary enjoyment of music involves the special creative powers of the great musicians.' How would this happen? – 'through an educative process; a drill'. If a person could learn how to practice the law or be good at business, so they could learn the mystic way. 'The education of the mystical self lies in self-simplification.'[7]

The mystic way, as she expounded it in the books she wrote in these years before she definitively returned to the Church of England, was largely an individual endeavour. This practical mysticism is a solo activity, and nowhere in the book does she mention churchgoing or corporate worship. In 1924, she wrote that she regarded the book as 'incomplete' because of its inattention to 'Institutional and Social spirituality'.[8] To one of her correspondents, she wrote that she was 'apt to be disagreeable on the Church question. I stood out against it myself for so long and have been so thoroughly convinced of my own error that I do not want other people to waste time in the same way … I do not mean that perpetual churchgoing and sermons are necessary, but some participation in the common religious life and sacramental life.'[9]

Nevertheless, we should not underestimate the influence that the little book *Practical Mysticism* – for all its failings, which she pointed out – had on people. James Lumsden Barkway, a Presbyterian who converted to Anglicanism and was Bishop of Bedford and then Bishop of St Andrew's, wrote of the impact that book had on him when he was given a copy in 1914 when it was published.

> I had been prepared for its message by many years of searching without finding and it spoke straight to the heart of my condition ... I had previously read Evelyn Underhill's two longer books, *Mysticism* and *The Mystic Way*, and had been greatly interested. But the intimate appeal of the smaller volume, with its characteristically homely illustrations, spoke to me ... directly ... Evelyn Underhill threw open a door before which I had been standing all my life, longing to get through. She encouraged me to make the experiment which the previous guides of my university and theological college days ... had said was beyond human capacity; and she assured me that direct and first-hand knowledge of God was not only desirable but possible.

For Lumsden Barkway, Underhill wrote in a way that was 'pertinent and relevant to the life of to-day.' She did this by practical common sense, and being unafraid to appeal to her own experience in prayer. This made her a very approachable spiritual director, as we shall explore later in this chapter.[10]

Responding to Seekers

Underhill always wanted to appeal to those who were searching, like the young Lumsden Barkway, and she recognized that there were increasing numbers of people who were alienated by and from institutional religion. In my Introduction to this book I quoted from her 1921 Upton Lectures, delivered in Oxford and written just after she had returned to the Anglican fold: 'I think we may now say without exaggeration that the general modern judgment – not, of course, the clerical or orthodox judgment – is adverse to institutionalism; at least as it now exists.' In those lectures, she explored what institutional religion can provide (as she had just embraced the Church of England this is perhaps not surprising): group-consciousness, religious union, discipline, and culture. And she wrote that as far as 'the freelance' (as she called those outside the body of the church) gets any of those things, it is, ultimately, 'indirectly from some institutional sources.' But, she continued, 'the institution, since it represents the element of stability in life, does not give, and must not be expected to give, direct, spiritual experience; or any onward push towards novelty, freshness of discovery and interpretation in the spiritual sphere.' She was also clear-eyed about the potential 'dangers and limitations' of institutional religion. It would generally dislike freshness of discovery, and would exalt the corporate and stable and discount the mobile and individual. 'Its natural instinct will be for exclusivism, the club-idea, conservatism and cosiness; it will, if left to itself, revel in the middle-aged atmosphere and exhibit the middle-aged point of view.'[11]

In this same year, 1921, she first went to the modernist layman Baron von Hügel for spiritual direction, and she was clearly trying to find a balance between engagement with corporate worship, now that she was committed to the church, and the more individual or personal form of spirituality that had hitherto been her main form of worship. He observed this about her: 'As a matter of fact I fear as much for you the overdoing of institutionalism as the ignoring or even flying from it: indeed, these two extremes are assuredly twin sisters in a soul such as yours.' He went on to say that he recommended 'a certain minimum, a nucleus of institutional practice, to which you will then adhere with a patient perseverance.' He perceived that 'this nucleus should not be fixed as for a naturally institutional soul, or even as for an average soul, but for your soul, which to the end will find the institutional more or less difficult, but will none the less greatly require some little of it faithfully performed.'[12] Underhill followed this advice and often passed a version of it on to others under her direction. For example, she wrote to one, in 1925:

> You aren't and never will be a real 'institutional soul' and are not required by God to behave like one. Your religion must of course have some institutional element, but it is particularly important that this element should not be overdone; and it certainly is not to be used as a penance.[13]

Underhill came to see the importance of this balance of the 'twin sisters' of her soul. She wrote to a spiritual directee in 1937: 'The corporate and personal together make up the Christian ideal.'[14] As she grew older she became clearer that one really could not be 'just spiritual'; she came to believe that to *grow* in one's relationship with God one had to have a firm rooting in a religious tradition. She wrote in 1934 to a new spiritual directee as follows:

I have been during my life (I am now approaching 60) through many phases of religious belief and I now realize – have done in fact for some time – that human beings can make little real progress on a basis of vague spirituality. God and the soul, and prayer as the soul's life, and the obligation of responding to God's demand, are real facts – in fact the most real of all facts – and they are facts with which orthodox religion deals.[15]

It is worth note that the last big book she wrote was *Worship*, in 1936, at the suggestion of Walter Matthews, Dean of St Paul's Cathedral. Here she writes about the transformative power of the sacraments – and corporate ritual and ceremonial generally – in a person's spiritual development.

But she continued to have deep empathy with, and concern for, those outside institutional religion who were seeking. Her friend, the poet T. S. Eliot, on whom her writing about mysticism was a great influence, said of her that she understood the 'grievous need of the contemplative element in the modern world.'[16] She had written in 1912, while she was still on the margins of the church: 'There's a lot of religious loneliness about.'[17]

She was also gentle with her spiritual directees as they began to grapple with faith, and understood that a beginner could not take on all the doctrines of the Church at once. She continued to that same new spiritual directee (referred to above):

As to dogmas which you cannot accept – e.g. the Virgin Birth – it is useless to force yourself on these points. Leave them alone for the time being, neither affirming nor rejecting them, and give your mind and will to living in harmony with those truths which you *do* see. This is the way – in fact the only way – to further light.[18]

She remained glad of her relatively marginal position – as a layperson and a woman – in the Church. She wrote to a correspondent in 1932, by which time she had been warmly incorporated into the Church of England and was active on committees and in retreat directing: 'it is one of the advantages of being a scamp, that one is unable to crystallize into the official shape, and so retains touch with other freelances and realizes how awful the ecclesiastical attitude and atmosphere often makes them feel.' Her perception of the ways in which the Church could be unwelcoming strikes a chord in our own day, as does her advice to her correspondent: 'As to feeling rather dismayed by the appearance of the Church Visible at the moment – that is inevitable I'm afraid to some extent. But keep your inner eye on the Church Invisible – what the Baron used to call "the great centralities of religion".'[19]

Spiritual Direction and Retreats

I have, for several years now, made a Lenten practice of reading Evelyn Underhill's *Letters* over 40 days.[20] I recommend Charles Williams' compilation of Underhill's letters, published in 1943, two years after her death, for this purpose. It is not scholarly and not complete, but it is a good introduction to the wisdom of this down-to-earth woman, small enough to put in your pocket – and you can easily pick up a second-hand copy.[21]

If I begin with her advice for Lenten practices, to one of her spiritual directees, you will perhaps see why the letters are so charming and appealing:

> As to your Lent – no physical hardships beyond what normal life provides – but take each of these as serenely and humbly as you can and make of them your humble offering to God. Don't reduce sleep. Don't get up in the cold. Practise more diligently the art of turning to God with some glance or phrase of love and trust at all spare moments in the day. Read a devotional book in bed in the morning, and strive in every way to make the ordinary discipline of life of spiritual worth. Be especially kind and patient with those who irritate you![22]

This is very typical of Underhill's advice: warm, gentle, and completely practical – she always emphasized the ordinariness of spiritual practice, and guarded against the temptation to try and be perfect. The life of prayer should not be a strain, as she wrote to another spiritual directee: 'Take things a bit more "as they come" – do all you can in a spirit of love and quite peacefully say to God, "I'm very sorry I did not make a better job of it." After all, if you did make a miraculously good job of it that might not fall within His plan for you, and might even bring with it a subtle temptation against humility.'[23]

She also had the measure of those she directed. To that same spiritual directee, who always wanted to take on deliberate hardships as part of an ascetic discipline, she wrote:

> As to deliberate mortifications – I take it you do feel satisfied that you accept fully those God sends? That

being so, you might perhaps do one or two little things, as acts of love, and also as discipline? I suggest by preference the mortification of the Tongue – as being very tiresome and quite harmless to the health. Careful guard on all amusing criticisms of others, on all complaints however casual and trivial; deliberately refraining sometimes (not *always!*) from saying the entertaining thing. This does not mean you have to be dull or correct! But to ration this side of your life. I doubt whether things like sitting on the least comfortable chair, etc., affect you enough to be worth bothering about! But I'm sure custody of the Tongue (on the lines suggested) could give you quite a bit of trouble and be a salutary bit of discipline, a sort of verbal hair-shirt.[24]

There is something in the giving of this advice that illustrates Underhill's capacity to catch the essence of someone or something and even be humorous about it. She had an eagle eye for the witty phrase that would make an idea or doctrine clear to her reader, writing for example that the reign of God is 'not merely a neat, benevolent and hygienic social order (the Baron [von Hügel] used to say "the Holy Spirit is not a sanitary Inspector") but the transfiguration of the world and of life into something consistent with God's will, which is the aim of redemption.'[25] Underhill had a sense of humour and an acute sense of the ironic and absurd, even at her own expense, as this description of going to lead a quiet day in 1934 suggests:

I had 100 clergy wives … No one told me there was Mass at the Cathedral, and the bell rang while I was in my bath, but I arrived, damp, just after the Gospel, and found NO one connected with the Quiet day there ... Well, then I had them from 11 to 5 in a frowsty little church, and we had ham sandwiches for lunch being Friday; and all felt it was a Wonderful and Devotional Day. And I got back to London 10:30 p.m. feeling that was that.[26]

By the mid-1920s, two or three years after she had settled into the Church of England, she was becoming a regular leader of such quiet days and retreats. She particularly loved doing this at the retreat house at Pleshey in Essex: it felt homely and normal to her, and it was the place where she made her first retreat as she was becoming a committed Anglican in 1921, and where she led her first retreat in 1924. She wrote to a friend, 'I have just been asked to conduct a three-day retreat at my dear Pleshey in Lent ... It seems a great responsibility, but I think I have to do it.'[27] She had been asked to conduct this retreat by a recent acquaintance – later a great friend – Dorothy Swayne, who at that time was Warden of the Time and Talents Settlement House, a hotel for women, in the impoverished area of Bermondsey in London. Swayne recorded that Underhill's 'whole face lit up, and she said that to conduct a retreat was something she had longed to do, but that so far she had not been given the opportunity.'[28] Swayne was, like Underhill later, a spiritual directee of Reginald Somerset Ward, whom we shall encounter in the next chapter.

The retreat house at Pleshey had been built in 1909 and taken over by the Diocese of Chelmsford in 1927 when the nuns left. It was made popular largely because of Underhill's work, to the extent that they were even able to build a new chapel in 1933, a description of which Underhill wrote for the

Church Times. Her friend Lucy Menzies was Warden at Pleshey from 1928 to 1938 and worked tirelessly to make it a special and welcoming place.

In fact, it was not only Pleshey that Underhill helped to make known, but retreats for a wider audience altogether, especially laypeople. In this growth of retreat-taking, the revival of interest in mysticism joined with Anglo-Catholicism and the re-establishment of monastic orders in the Anglican Church (which had begun in the nineteenth century). Some of those monastic orders had encouraged retreat-taking, and a pioneer in this was Richard Benson, founder of the Society of St John the Evangelist (SSJE) in Cowley in Oxford, who had written a tract on retreats in 1865. The opening up of retreats to a much wider group of people began in earnest in 1913, just a decade before Underhill joined the work, when the Association for Short Retreats was founded, later renamed the Association for Promoting Retreats. The clergy and lay women who led this movement were inspired not only by the Anglican monastics, but also by the work of a young Jesuit, Charles Plater, who published *Retreats for the People* in 1912, which reflected on his visits to France and Belgium where such work was underway. There was a push to get every diocese in the Church of England to have a retreat house, where it would be possible for any woman or man – not just the all-male clergy – to have a quiet day or two. When World War I ended, it was felt that retreat houses could play a part in the rehabilitation of the demobbed, especially those who were suffering from injuries and shell-shock, and in 1919 there were retreats at Pleshey designed especially for those returning from the war. The

Association for Promoting Retreats kept statistics, and the number of guided-retreats in England increased from 185 in 1920 to 470 in 1934.

In an address to the Association for Promoting Retreats, Underhill articulated the 'need for retreat.' She spoke of 'its power of causing the re-birth of our spiritual sense, quickening that which has grown dull and dead in us, calling it into the light and air, giving it another chance.' She was aware of the ways in which our busy, noisy lives prevent us from taking time to 'rest in the Lord'. Then 'we lose all sense of proportion;' we become 'restless, fussy, full of things that simply must be done, quite oblivious of the only reason anything should be done.' A retreat was therefore an opportunity to learn and maintain 'the art of steadfast attention to God.'[29]

However, Underhill was unusual as a female, lay retreat leader. In 1924, the Society of Retreat Conductors was formed, to train retreat leaders and help administer retreat houses to a high standard. Both this group and the Association for Promoting Retreats were run by the Anglo-Catholic Congress, which debated whether laypeople, and especially women (all of whom were lay then, of course) should be trained as retreat conductors. The answer was a firm no. Male priests were to retain a monopoly on this vocation (though mother superiors might lead only their own nuns in a retreat). It was thought that women would not have the necessary authority.

Evelyn Underhill was therefore the great exception to these guidelines and, paradoxically, probably the best-known (and now most-remembered) leader of retreats in the Church of the time. She was therefore a pioneer – as well as a pioneering woman - in this field. In 1924, the Dean of Canterbury, George Bell (later Bishop of Chichester) invited her to take a retreat at the cathedral – the first woman to do so. Underhill even led retreats for the clergy (not just the clergy wives of the ham sandwich incident related earlier). She often began her addresses to the clergy in a self-effacing way, and then said exactly what needed to be said in her usual kind and direct fashion. In 1936, she led the retreat for the clergy of the Diocese of Worcester, and began in typical fashion:

> It seems presumptuous for anyone, and especially a member of the laity, to attempt to add to that which has already been said and written upon the spiritual life of the Christian priest. Only the overwhelming importance of the subject for the work of the Church, and the fact that in the pressure of outward life we need again and again to be reminded of those unchanging realities of the inward life which alone can give any value to our active work can justify this.

She then went on to remind the gathered clergy that while things such as intellectual and social aptitude, good preaching, and a capacity for organization were all helpful for the work of a priest, none of those was essential. The only thing essential is prayer. 'The man whose life is coloured by prayer, whose loving communion with God comes first, will always win souls; because he shows them in his own life and person the attractiveness of reality, the demand, the transforming power of the spiritual life.' It therefore follows that 'the priest's life of prayer… is not only his primary obligation to the Church; it is the only condition under which the work of Christian ministry can be properly done.' Only prayer could support the most difficult of ministries, in the toughest of circumstances. 'To do great things for souls, you must become the channel of a more than human love; and this must be the chief object of the priest's life of prayer.'[30] From this exhortation to put prayer first, Underhill then turned – as always – to the practicalities. She knew that a priest's time was limited because of his obligations, and so she reminded the gathered clergy of their obligation to say the morning and evening office every day, which should be the frame of their praying life. She also reminded them that in their work of developing the latent spiritual tendencies of their parishioners, their own praying life as a model was again primary, ahead of what went on in the parish and the formation of small prayer groups, both of which she recommended heartily.

Every year, in re-reading the Letters during Lent, I notice something different. This year, I observed more acutely Underhill's development as a spiritual director, the ways in which she began tentatively and became more sure-footed. In 1907 when people first began to write to her, having read her novels (*Mysticism* did not come out for another four years) she wrote to her husband that having to help people out of their spiritual tangles was 'a most horrible responsibility and rather ridiculous when the person applied to is still in just as much of a tangle as everyone else.'[31] But help them she did, offering the reading she had found useful, encouraging them along on the basis of her own experience of praying, affirming the validity of 'direct spiritual experience, ' and encouraging them to trust it, when other people they had consulted had said that what they had found was not there at all. Underhill was always a witness to the there-ness of Reality with a capital R, inviting others to experience it.

By the 1920s and 30s, she was a mature Christian and seasoned spiritual director who helped people through their dry periods, always inviting them to walk through the fog; say the offices dully and coldly if necessary for it is not how we feel about them that matters, but *that* we do them, for God is acting in us. 'Keep quiet inwardly and let God act,' she wrote to one spiritual directee. 'Don't be worried. It is God you want and God wants you.'[32]

There is no doubt that Underhill was a pioneer – she frequently found herself the first woman (and sometimes the first layperson) to do what she was doing in church and university contexts. Interestingly, she was opposed to the ordination of women – in contrast with Percy Dearmer and Reginald Somerset Ward who, as we shall see, were supportive of women's ordained ministry – because she felt, as an Anglo-Catholic, that she was part of a larger Catholic whole that could only act together on such a matter.[33]

People who met Underhill found her charming and unassuming though there was also a radiance about her. A friend described visiting her in 1937, after she had suffered one of the illnesses that plagued her towards the end of her life (she died in 1941). 'As I entered she got up and turned round, so fragile as though a puff of wind might blow her away... but light simply streamed from her face illuminated with a radiant smile. ... One could not but feel consciously there and then ... that one was in the presence of the extension of the

Mystery of our Lord's Transfiguration in one of the members of His Mystical body.'[34]

What most stands out about Evelyn Underhill is her practical spirituality: she often told her spiritual directees not to make a fuss. She had the unshakeable belief that there is 'a real transcendental spark in us' which, once it is awakened, 'can only be satisfied by God.'[35] Once that desire for a relationship with the divine had been awoken, it will grow as quickly as God wills, without us fussing about it. She described the spiritual life as like a bowl of spring bulbs that one puts under the bed to grow during the winter months – one should not keep getting the bulbs out and prodding them to see how they are doing.[36]

Her life's work was to help people to that awakening, to let them know that a prayer life was possible for anyone and to coach them gently towards the mystic way or life *in* God.

Notes

1   On this revival of interest in mysticism in the early twentieth century, see Jane Shaw, 'Varieties of Mystical Experience in William James and other Moderns', *History of European Ideas* (Vol. 43, Issue 3, 2017), pp. 226 – 240

2   W. R. Inge, *Christian Mysticism* (London: Methuen and Co., 1899), pp. 329 – 330

3   W. R. Inge, *Mysticism in Religion* (London: Hutchinson's University Library, 1947), p. 135

4   Letter to Mrs Meyrick Heath, 14 May 1911, in *The Letters of Evelyn Underhill*, ed. Charles Williams (London: Longmans, Green and Co., [1943] 5th edition 1945), p. 126

5   Evelyn Underhill, *Mysticism. A Study in the Nature and Development of Man's Spiritual Consciousness* (1911) (London: Methuen & Co., [8th edition] 1918), pp. 28, x

6   *Collected Papers of Evelyn Underhill*, ed. Lucy Menzies (London: Longmans, Green and Co., 1946), pp. 107, 107 – 8, 108 – 9

7   Evelyn Underhill, *Practical Mysticism* (1914) (New York: Dover Books, 2000), pp. 6, 15

8   *Letters*, ed. Williams, p. 152

9   Quoted in Margaret Cropper, *The Life of Evelyn Underhill* (1958) (Woodstock, VT: Skylight Paths Publishing, 2003), p. 70

10 James Lumsden Barkway, 'Introduction,' *Collected Papers*, ed. Menzies, pp. 7 – 8

11 Underhill, *Life of the Spirit*, pp. 125 – 6

12 Quoted in Cropper, *The Life of Evelyn Underhill*, p. 71

13 *Letters*, ed. Williams, p. 169

14 *Letters* ed. Williams, p. 261

15 *Letters*, ed. Williams, p. 239

16 Quoted by Dana Greene in her 'Introduction' to Evelyn Underhill, *Modern Guide to the Ancient Quest for the Holy*, ed. Dana Greene (Albany NY: SUNY Press, 1988), p. 2

17 *Letters*, ed. Williams, p. 140

18 *Letters*, ed. Williams, pp. 239 – 40

19 *Letters*, ed. Williams, p. 207

20 My short Lenten book *A Practical Christianity* (New York: Morehouse Publishing and London: SPCK, 2012) is, at some level, a response to this practice of reading Underhill's letters once a year, and its title is a deliberate play on Underhill's book title, *Practical Mysticism.*

21 For an excellent modern, critical edition, see *The Making of a Mystic: New and Selected Letters of Evelyn Underhill,* ed. Carol Poston (Urbana and Chicago: The University of Illinois Press, 2010)

22 *Letters,* ed. Williams, p. 252

23 *Letters,* ed. Williams, p. 244

24 *Letters,* ed. Williams, p. 259

25 *Letters,* ed. Williams, p. 222

26 *Letters,* ed. Williams, p. 235

27 *Letters,* ed. Williams, p. 150

28 Cropper, *The Life of Evelyn Underhill,* p. 122. The Time and Talents Association was an Anglican group set up in 1895 by middle class women to help young working girls and women.

29 Evelyn Underhill, 'The Need of Retreat', originally published in *The Vision* in January 1932 and reprinted in Evelyn Underhill, *The Light of Christ. Retreats at the House of Retreat, Pleshey, May 1932* (London, New York and Toronto: Longmans, Green and Co., 1944), pp. 102, 107

30 *Collected Papers,* ed. Menzies, pp. 121, 122, 127

31 *Letters,* ed. Williams, p. 61

32 *Letters,* ed. Williams, p. 231

33 For her arguments against the ordination of women, see 'The Ideals of the Ministry of Women', *Theology* 26, No. 151 (1933), pp. 37 – 42. Annice Callahan, a Roman Catholic nun, thinks that Underhill may have been swayed in favour of the ordination of women if she were living in our own day: 'above all, for the sake of the mission of the Church, which is the proclamation of Christ.' Annice Callahan, *Evelyn Underhill: Spirituality for Daily Living* (Lanham, MD: University Press of America, 1997), p. 215

34 *Letters,* ed. Williams, p. 37

35 *Letters,* ed. Williams, p. 241

36 *Letters,* ed. Williams, p. 169

Chapter 2

Reginald Somerset Ward
Prayer

From 1933, Evelyn Underhill's spiritual director was an Anglican priest named Reginald Somerset Ward. He was one of the most influential spiritual directors of the first half of the twentieth century, though not well-known as a figure in the church. He kept his work hidden and published his books anonymously to avoid spiritual pride and competition. It was at his Memorial Service in Westminster Abbey, in 1962, that the full impact of his ministry became obvious: a great crowd of Anglicans gathered, many of them holding high office in the Church; none of them knew who else had been his spiritual directees and one can imagine them turning to each other and thinking, 'Oh, you - and you and you!' The stewards, surprised at the crowds at the service, asked, 'What manner of man was this?' The Dean of Westminster, Eric Symes Abbott, said in the Bidding Prayer: 'We thank God openly for a priest whose ministry was hidden.'[1]

Nevertheless, Ward has been brought to a little public attention in recent years. Eagle-eyed readers of Susan

Howatch's 'Starbridge' novels, which take place in a fictionalised Salisbury Cathedral Close, may remember that Ward is quoted from time to time in her novel *Absolute Truths*, which explores one of her main recurring characters in the series, Charles Ashworth. By now a bishop, Ashworth is, in this novel, on the search for truth in the wake of his wife's death, and apt quotations from Reginald Somerset Ward serve as epigraphs, framing that search. Howatch opens the book with a quotation from Ward's book *To Jerusalem*: 'Absolute Truth is a very uncomfortable thing when we come into contact with it. For the most part, in daily life, we get along more easily by avoiding it; not by deceit, but by running away from it ....' Later, just before Ashworth is about to go to bed with a woman to whom he is not married, Howatch places this quotation from Ward's book *The Way* at the beginning of the chapter: 'We learn by the bitter experience of temptation that the spiritual life is not a matter of devout feeling or the mere desire to be good....'[2] Ward's work *To Jerusalem*, published in 1931, was reissued in 1994, with his name as author on the cover this time, and an introduction by Susan Howatch.

I should also say by way of introduction that Ward is a very serious, even austere, character; it is hard to find a witty line in Ward's writings (a sharp contrast with Evelyn Underhill and Rose Macaulay), or a love of beauty and art (in contrast with Percy Dearmer). Ward's honesty and dedication shine through, but he was even serious about taking leisure time. In a snapshot of him sitting in a deckchair on the beach with his wife, he is deeply earnest as he looks straight at the camera.[3]

So, who was this man? Reginald Somerset Ward always sat rather lightly to the institutional church; in fact, it may be fair to say that he did not really like it, though it was very much a part of him. Born in 1881 (six years younger than Evelyn Underhill), he was the son of a Church of England vicar, educated at Cambridge and ordained in 1904. In 1906, he married an American, Charlotte Kissam. He served two curacies and then in 1909 became Secretary of the Sunday School Institute. By this time, he had begun to be aware of a new reality in his own prayer life, and was reading Julian of Norwich, Teresa of Avila, and other mystical writers, and having mystical experiences which he discussed with his own spiritual director, one Father Vaughan. In 1913, he became the Rector of Chiddingford, and it quickly became obvious that he was not cut out to be a parish priest: not least, preaching pacifism in the parish after World War I broke out did not make him popular. And then, in 1915, he received what he perceived as a very strong call from God, in prayer, to give himself up to the work of spiritual direction. 'I believe that God has called me to do other work and to do it under other circumstances' he announced to his parish from the pulpit, having defined vocation as 'the voice of God.' He went on in that sermon: 'It is the direct, clear, personal Voice of God, singling out that one individual from the millions of the world and communicating to him or her that absolute Will of the Supreme Father. You can argue about a Vocation; you can say it is self-deception, or delusion, or mania, but you cannot argue with it. When it comes, the soul who receives it has but one possible answer – that of obedience.'[4]

Despite his dislike of institutions, he did indeed believe in obedience, so he went to his bishop, Edward Talbot of

Winchester, who advised him to follow the call. He resigned from the parish, not knowing how he would support himself, his wife and their two children, but with faith. Soon afterwards, a friend told him that anonymous persons would provide sufficient means for him to live on. And so, the Ward family moved to a house called Ravenscroft in Farncombe in Surrey, where they remained for the rest of their lives. A room at the top of the house became a chapel, licensed by Bishop Talbot, who then placed Ward under the supervision of the Suffragan Bishop of Guildford. Ward occasionally preached and helped out at the parish church in Farncombe, but he was now essentially a 'free lance' as Underhill would have put it, albeit under obedience to a bishop. Ward was able to develop his distinctive ministry of spiritual direction.

Spiritual Direction, Prayer and The Road

Ward dedicated the rest of his life to spiritual direction. He eventually came to have about two hundred spiritual directees. He saw them four times a year, for a clearly defined period, usually half an hour each, traveling to different cities in England on his spiritual direction 'tours.' He had different centres where he met people: London, Newcastle, Carlisle, Leeds, Carnforth, Liverpool, Bristol, Cardiff, Cheltenham, Birmingham. Derby, Bournemouth, Winchester, and Tunbridge Wells. He saw about twelve people per day. He began the spiritual direction sessions by asking, 'How are things going?' and 'Any sense of reality in your prayers?' The short session ended with hearing the person's confession if they wished, and a blessing. Ward's was an intense and demanding schedule, with travel on trains and sleep in a different hotel every night; he reduced the number of tours he took to three times a year in 1925, and he had to bring these extensive tours to an end in 1947 when he was 66 years old. But he continued to see people in his home in Farncombe, and in London, up until his death in 1962, aged 81.

He took the work of spiritual direction with the utmost seriousness, for he believed that in order for Christians to be useful, especially spiritually useful, they had to know themselves. And spiritual direction could greatly assist an individual in that self-examination. He wrote: 'What is needed above all for God's kingdom on earth is quality. Quantity will take care of itself if we take care of quality. … Those who have a real desire and passion to help others must, of necessity, first attack their own lives and find in them the tool they can use to help others. The missionary spirit without the spiritual life is helpless.'[5]

One of his great followers was the Anglican priest Norman Goodacre, who wrote of his experience of these spiritual direction sessions: 'RSW never just "heard confessions". Always there were two chairs … he sat with his penitent and the session was one of reconciliation with emphasis on counsel, healing, training, forgiveness, and new life. Half an hour is a short time, but he was recognized as a "master of diagnosis"; his direction was severely simple and sternly practical. As one obituary put it, "his strictness was formidable but never marred by legalism and always tempered by humility and compassion".' Some people found him alarming. Goodacre wrote, 'For some penitents he was too severe and too dogmatic, but never for me. I found him utterly understanding, strong in direction, skilled in counsel, and versed in the heights and depths of prayer. It was a spiritual experience in itself to have a session with him.'[6] One directee, Miss Magdalen Liddle, recorded that he was mostly kind and compassionate, but he could be harsh and even – at least seemingly – unsympathetic at times which she understood as her own need of 'bracing.'[7]

At the heart of everything Ward did, and all of his spiritual direction, was prayer. In his book *To Jerusalem* (1931), Ward laid out three categories of prayer. The first is vocal prayer, which entails using written prayers (the Lord's Prayer being 'the standard'); all liturgy fitted into this category, including the Eucharist and the other sacraments. The second is intellectual or devotional reading, in which one could 'catch again the breath of God enclosed in human word.' And finally, there was mental or contemplative prayer; of this he wrote: 'this way of praying is like a very close sort of conversation, where all the explanations and forms which make conversation so cumbrous are left out, because both parties understand them.' It was life-giving, because it was, said Ward, the closest form of contact with God for learning; the truly vivifying channel of growth. He found that each person is usually drawn to one of these forms of prayer more than the other two, and he believed that one of his roles was to help each person develop the areas of prayer on which they did not naturally focus.[8] (This is in contrast with Underhill, who had a more gentle sense that her directees should focus on the ways in which they *could* pray.)

Ward himself had mystical experiences in prayer. Underhill, at least as a younger woman, defined mysticism as the essence of all religion, not just Christianity, even if her frame became distinctly Christian. By contrast, Ward's mysticism was always fully Christian in its expression: 'the Incarnate life of the Beloved [Jesus] is reflected and re-enacted in each mystical soul.' For Ward, to engage in this reflecting and re-enacting – to live the mystic life – we have to rely on the Beloved, namely Jesus. This means that 'the Life upon which mystical faith is dependent is one of sacrament and prayer, and without these two it slips back, step by step, to doubt.' It is worth noting here the emphasis on the sacraments.[9]

A rule of prayer is therefore necessary, said Ward, because the soul 'cannot trust itself to unrestricted nature in communicating with God to Whom it is so closely united. The things of this world and of the senses are so much more real to the poor, blind soul than God, that it will occupy all its time with them and suffer every kind of distraction from them if it has not some outside strength to succour it.' A rule also ensures regularity. 'The growth of the soul must be steady; it cannot grow by fits and starts.'[10] As an example of a rule of prayer, he suggested: two hours of prayer a day; always mid-day prayer if possible; prayer four times a day; a verse of Scripture for the purpose of mystical meditation, initially for ten minutes; two days each year for a retreat.[11] Ward admitted, from personal experience, that even though long habit made it natural to keep the Rule of Prayer, the 'principle of putting prayer first in daily life' did not necessarily become any easier to keep. 'The drawing in of our thoughts, the concentration on God, the efforts of attention, are all steps which require time.' Nevertheless, he wrote, 'My experience of life teaches me still the same lesson I received at first – that the Rule of Prayer is the master-key of life.'[12]

Ward did not believe that this path of disciplined prayer – which was for him the path to mystical union with God, which was 'Jerusalem' - was for everyone. This Rule of Life, which put prayer first, was a vocation – an important concept for Ward – and in this he differed from Underhill who believed that anyone could be a mystic. He began *To Jerusalem* by reminding his readers of the first disciples on the night of the Last Supper, and the betrayal and arrest of Jesus.

> For remember, there were two classes of people in the world that Thursday night – the multitude and the disciples. The former knew little or nothing of Christ and made no protestations; the latter knew much and said with exceeding vehemence, 'If we must die with Thee, we will not deny Thee.' And we before God claim to belong, or desire to belong, to that second class. We protest that we desire to follow, and be taught by, our Lord Jesus Christ. So in the light of the events of that night I would ask you to face the meaning and the cost of being a disciple of our Lord.

To live, truly live as a disciple, one had to learn humility, and 'humility comes of knowledge. Knowledge of two persons – God and oneself. The only way in which we shall ever be strong enough to be disciples is by being humble; the only way we can be truly humble is by knowing God and ourselves.'[13]

Ward formed a group for those who declared their wish to be disciples in this way; they were described as being on The Road (or The Way); this was neither an order nor a society but a training in mystical prayer. People were admitted with the words: 'By the authority committed into me I admit thee to the Road, in the name of the Father, and of the Son, and of the Holy Ghost. Amen.' The register of those on The Road suggests that the vast majority of lay people engaged in this were women, alongside a good number of priests and deaconesses.

The very first person who joined The Road with Ward was Deaconess Phyllis Dent, with whom Ward had worked at the Sunday School Institute, and who helped him understand his own spiritual leanings. Ward always supported deaconesses, and he had several them under his direction. In 1923, Bishop Talbot appointed Ward as the Warden of the Deaconess House of St Andrew's in Portsmouth, and so he gathered around him a small group of deaconesses and advocated for great visibility and resources for the work of deaconesses nationally.

The members of The Road formed not a church but what we might describe as a dispersed community; they were reassured in the tough spiritual work of The Road that they had fellow travelers. The work of The Road spread throughout and beyond Britain, through different parts of the Anglican Communion: in South Africa, India, Australia, Jamaica and the USA. Sub-groups of The Road were formed in these places, overseen by key priests. Norman Goodacre, who succeeded Ward as Director of The Road from 1962 (the year that Ward died), kept a register of all who had joined The Road, and by 1978, the total number came to 431, of whom 225 had been directed by Ward himself, another 99 by Goodacre. The numbers were not, therefore, large – as might be expected by this hidden ministry. Its growth depended on word of mouth and networks as the following brief examples illustrate.

Magdalen Liddle, whose reactions to Ward's spiritual direction I mentioned briefly, joined when she was teaching music at the Diocesan Girls' School in Grahamstown, South Africa. She learnt about it from the Director of the South Africa group: the Revd Jasper Bazeley, who was chaplain to St Paul's Theological College and to the Diocesan School of Girls in Grahamstown where Miss Liddle was music teacher. She was admitted to The Road in 1916 by a telegram from Ward, which simply said: 'I admit you.'[14] She later went back to live in England, where Ward became her spiritual director. She was typical of the women – nurses, missionaries attached to churches, teachers and deaconesses – who were attracted to this disciplined Rule of Prayer. Another, based in England, was Miss Muriel Breary, who spent her entire life working for the Church, primarily as Sunday School organizer for the Diocese of Southwark. She ran a training centre for Sunday School teachers in Blackfriars and, during World War II, took a house to which people came for spiritual refreshment. Presumably, she learnt about The Road from Deaconess Phyllis Dent through the Sunday School Institute.

Dorothy Swayne was another such woman. The daughter of a bishop, educated at Oxford, she went on to train as a social worker. In 1919, she became Warden of the Time and Talents Settlement at Bermondsey, and, in that capacity, was the person who invited Underhill to lead her first retreat, as we saw in Chapter 1. From there, Swayne went on to work for the

Diocese of Southwark as the Organising Secretary for Youth Work, and then became Warden of a new settlement house in Morden in the 1930s, at which point she became involved in developing the Third Order (Lay Order) of Franciscans in England and came under the spiritual direction of Reginald Somerset Ward, remaining so until 1961, just before his death. She was much supported and much influenced by Ward, especially in the notion of hiddenness, and she published her own books on prayer and meditation under the pseudonym 'Martha'. These books show the influence of Ward in the idea of traveling a road of prayer, encouraging regular time for prayer, and the notion of prayer as entering into the stream of God's love.[15]

While the numbers in The Road were relatively small, Ward's writings spread his message to a wider audience. The pastoral letters he wrote to those on The Road – especially those overseas – and the monthly instructions he circulated to his spiritual directees were subsequently published in a series of books: *The Way* (1922), *Following the Way* (1925), *To Jerusalem* (1931), *The Way in Prayer* (1932) and *Prayer in Lent* (1956). In addition, we should remember that his spiritual direction of a wide array of people led to his influence being spread through their work: they were priests (including such prominent figures as Michael Ramsey, who became Archbishop of Canterbury) as well as deaconesses and laypeople who were prominent and active in the work of the church. He therefore guided the prayer life of many at the heart of the church, and through his spiritual discernment helped those people in their ministry. Ward was himself a member of a small cell of priests which formed in 1937, gathering regularly to discuss their prayer lives and their concern about the training of priests. This group included Leslie Owen, who was then Warden of Lincoln Theological College and subsequently became Bishop of Jarrow, of Maidstone and finally of Lincoln; Lumsden Barkway, then Bishop of Bedford and later Bishop of St Andrews (whom we encountered in chapter 1); and Eric Symes Abbott, then Principal of the Bishop's Hostel at Lincoln and later Dean of King's College, London, Warden of Keble College, Oxford, and finally Dean of Westminster Abbey.[16]

The aim of The Road

Like Underhill, Ward had a sense of our thirst for God – implanted there by God: 'He put into man's soul that unquenchable spark which will for ever soar upwards.' It is something greater than ourselves that we are compelled to explore: 'there is something in us stronger than thought, deeper than consciousness, which continually aspires to reach out of us to some vast goal which cannot be contained in the tiny mirror of our minds.' This is Life – a 'vast stream of becoming.'[17] We long to seek the reality of God, and for Ward we do that through an intermediary, Jesus Christ, precisely because he is both God and human; and we carry out that search through our souls: namely, through prayer.

The aim of the life of prayer on The Road is to attain to such periods and amounts of union with God as God wills (*perpetual* conscious union with God not being possible in this life). The travelling of The Road is therefore the purging of the love of self, the crucifixion of self-will, accomplished by detachment, obedience and mortification. Obedience was central to Ward's scheme, and on entering The Road to Mystical Prayer, each person had to answer these questions (in the affirmative):

- Do you freely choose to follow this Road to God? If called by God to do so, are you prepared to give up all that you possess, all that you desire, and all that you hope for, in order to follow this Road to God?
- Are you prepared to undergo and offer to God suffering, humiliation, and the crucifixion of the soul, if called upon to do so?
- Are you willing to give your obedience to your director, subject to the four safeguards which follow?

We may note that the safeguards show Ward's humility, and the sense that, despite the hierarchical relationship between spiritual director and directee as embodied in the emphasis on obedience, all were under Christ's teaching and rule.

The safeguards were:

1. At any moment, without giving any reason, you are at liberty to write to your director withdrawing your obedience on your own, sole responsibility.
2. A command given under obedience which is clearly against the Ten Commandments or the Sermon on the Mount is null and void.
3. Any previous vow, promise or obligation, which is not clearly against the Ten Commandments or the Sermon on the Mount is left untouched by the obedience.

4. A reason may be demanded for any command under obedience.[18]

Retreats

Ward was a part of the movement encouraging retreat-taking in this period, and the Association for Promoting Retreats published a number of his retreat addresses (anonymously, as all his works were published). Preparation was an essential component of the spiritual path because, as Ward put it, 'Faith is no sudden outburst, but the result of training and preparation'.[19] This was especially the case on retreats because the care, effort and attention given to preparing for the retreat would determine the value of the retreat itself, and the degree to which divine aid and the person's cooperation would further the spiritual path during that time. The whole purpose of the retreat was to be with God, and Ward's suggested rules were always about the circumstances that would make that possible for the retreatant. For example:

1. The soul in retreat is to take two periods of one hour each day for recreation, one of these if possible is to be spent in the open air.
2. At least eight hours are to be set aside for sleep.
3. At least three meals are to be taken during the day with this exception, such abstinence as is found most useful may be used.
4. One act of charity (writing a letter, alms, act of kindness) must be offered to God each day.
5. Absolute silence is to be observed subject to any exceptions dictated by common sense.

6. No vow or resolution made at the end of the retreat shall be held to be binding until it has received the sanction of the Director.

7. Not more than three of such services as are held daily in the place of retreat need be attended by the soul in retreat.

8. The programme of the retreat is simply a suggested outline and not binding either as to order or duration.

9. No letters should be opened or read during retreat.[20]

The last suggestion would now be changed to: don't look at your phone, social media or emails.

Ward gave a series of addresses on a theme at his retreats, each followed by a period of silent prayer so that the retreatants could reflect on what had been said. There then followed a verse of scripture upon which there would be some meditation by each individual (which was one of the types of prayer he advised for his directees). This might be followed by an exercise – such as this exercise in trust:

Consider

1. *WHAT you are*: one tiny soul in the midst of millions, wholly unable to achieve any spiritual goal unaided or to accomplish your desire by your own power.

2. *WHERE you are*: at a certain spot in the midst of your life; not by chance, but by God's arrangement and will; for a certain definite purpose known to him.

3. *HOW you are to use this day*: by allowing God to carry out His will and purpose; cooperating with Him by sheer trust in His promise and intention for you.[21]

A book was usually set for the retreat, with recommended chapters for reading each day (such as Julian of Norwich's *Revelations of Divine Love*). At the end of the retreat, the retreatants were each to write out what they had learnt in the Retreat; give thanksgiving for the retreat; offer worship in thanksgiving (for example, saying the Sanctus); and offer themselves to God that they might be used as God willed.

What may strike us about all of this – the Rule, the retreats, Ward's suggestions and directions in his writings – is how highly structured it is. And despite his constant refrain that everything is a cooperation between human beings and God, it is the case that human beings have to put a lot in. Take this comment of his on perseverance, which comes at the end of his book *To Jerusalem*: 'Of all the tests of the saint I suppose this is the hardest for us. To go on day by day without getting slack, without continual stimulus, is an awful task. Look back on life and you will see how often we have had the opportunities for sainthood, and how often we have lost them because we would not persevere. Yet this is certain, that there is no moment too late in life to begin the making of a saint; that if we now set ourselves to ignore self-will, to face humiliation and contempt and to persevere steadfastly, the way lies open which leads to the very throne of God.'[22]

We may be left wondering how much grace plays a role in his theological scheme. For Ward, even the acceptance of God's forgiveness of our sins requires some work on our part. He wrote in *The Way*: 'God's forgiveness of our sins requires certain preliminary activities on our part – confession, contrition, and amendment. We cannot be forgiven without

42

preparation, and therefore we are always forewarned of the spiritual experience of forgiveness. We should expect, for this reason, that our consciousness of forgiveness would be fuller than usual, and would make a deeper impression on life and character.' This consciousness of forgiveness is important, says Ward, though he admits that we may not attain it in times of spiritual darkness; but when we have it, the marks of it are a perception of freedom, and a sense of joy and lightheartedness. The balance between grace and works always seems to tip on the side of works for Ward: 'We may say truly that all consciousness lies in the gift of God, but after we have acknowledged this, we must recognize that our perception of any spiritual state may be greatly increased by our efforts.'[23]

Spiritual Adventure and a Rule of Life

On the other side of regulation, perseverance and obedience was adventure. Ward opened his book, *To Jerusalem*, with an invitation to adventure within the boundaries of our ordinary, everyday lives.

> To our normal mind, if we trouble to think about it, our daily life presents certain similarities to a prison. It is limited by certain conditions, necessities and rules which seem to prevent any great or marked change. We have to get through a fixed amount of work at definite times, and to be present at certain meals, and to get a regular amount of sleep. What opportunity is there in such an environment for adventure?

The mistake, he says, is in thinking there are only three dimensions in which we live; but there is, rather, a fourth dimension, that of the Spirit, in which the opportunities for exploration are endless. Every small thing we do has the potential for infinite variation according to our state of mind and attitude – because the Holy Spirit is acting in us. Every conversation is a potential adventure, capable of momentous results. All through the day, which seems so fixed and so ordinary avenues are continually presented to us for a journey into a far country. At every road we pass, there are miracles waiting around the corner.[24]

This sounds like the current vogue for mindfulness, eating each mouthful of food so that we really taste it, washing the dishes with attention. But I think it is more than that. Ward is pushing his directees here to discover the new and push their own limits into the new. He wrote: 'I cannot learn charity, that is love of my neighbour as God loves him, unless I make daily experiments. If I limit my efforts to what I have always done, my charity will be what it has always been.' (Perhaps this is a reflection of Jesus' injunction on forgiveness in Matthew 18:21-22, where Jesus tells Peter that he needs to forgive someone not seven times but seventy times seven?) And then: 'I cannot learn humility, that is, to see myself as God sees me, unless I am prepared to make and to take opportunities each day for new points of view, new insights into my motives and my thoughts.'[25] In other words, our relationship with God is just that: a *relationship*, which grows and changes over our lives.

We might sum all of this up by saying that Ward lived by the simple spiritual maxim that through discipline comes freedom (though that is my language rather than his). One of the ways in which this was most obvious is that he divided the waking day into three roughly equal portions: prayer, recreation and work, and he believed that they were of *that order in importance.* He advised this for all his spiritual directees. The rule of prayer thus becomes – when rounded out like this – a rule of life.

He followed this disciplined rule of life himself. He worked very hard as a spiritual director, maintaining a huge correspondence; he spent a portion of each day in prayer, and was strict about taking time off for recreation. It was perhaps typical of the man that recreation was subject to his spiritual discipline. He observed a day off a week for walking, rowing, watching cricket and his hobbies of bookbinding, making dolls' house furniture, writing poetry, and reading – especially later in life on archaeology. He said in an address to some of his directees: 'I would warn you against the sin of overwork.' He continued:

> Many of you seem to think it is right to misuse the strength God gives you. … Overwork among conscientious souls is a far more real and frequent sin than laziness, and we ought to be more ready to suspect it and guard against it than we are. You need eight hours in bed and one day a week free from work if you are to give God your best service. Are you securing this amount of rest? If you are not, there ought to be a very serious questioning of your consciences in this matter.'[26]

He said all of this not in the abstract, but from his own deep experience of overworking.

There is an echo here of what Underhill said in her address to the clergy of the Diocese of Worcester, quoted in the previous chapter.

The man whose life is coloured by prayer, whose loving communion with God comes first, will always win souls; because he shows them in his own life and person the attractiveness of reality, the demand, the transforming power of the spiritual life. It therefore follows that 'the priest's life of prayer... is not only his primary obligation to the Church; it is the only condition under which the work of Christian ministry can be properly done.

Only prayer could support the most difficult of ministries, in the toughest of circumstances. 'To do great things for souls, you must become the agent and channel of a more than human love; and this must be the chief object of the priest's life of prayer.'[27] It is perhaps not surprising that she wrote this in 1936 when she was under the spiritual direction of Reginald Somerset Ward herself.

Ward's writings and work as a spiritual director remind us of the importance of the disciplined prayer life in faith and, more broadly than that, a rule of life. We will explore that in relation to our own times in the final chapter.

We shift now from the importance of the private life of prayer to the public life of worship as envisioned by another pioneer of modern spirituality, Percy Dearmer.

Notes

1 *Reginald Somerset Ward 1881 – 1962: His Life and Letters*, ed. Edmund R. Morgan (London: Mowbray, 1963), pp. 42 – 43

2 Susan Howatch, *Absolute Truths* (New York: Alfred A. Knopf, 1995), pp. 1, 289

3 Reginald Somerset Ward (RSW) papers, Lambeth Palace Library (LPL), MS4134

4 RSW papers, LPL, MS4134

5 *Reginald Somerset Ward 1881 – 1962* ed. Morgan, p. 77. Morgan's 'Memoir' in this book provides biographical details about Ward.

6 RSW papers, LPL, MS4139

7 RSW papers, LPL, MS4168

8 A Priest [Reginald Somerset Ward], *To Jerusalem: Devotional Studies in Mystical Religion* (London: The S. Christopher Press, 1931), pp. 118, 119

9 Ward, 'Retreat on Mysticism' pp. 28, 26, RSW papers, LPL, MS4134

10 Ward, 'A Little Treatise on Prayer' in typewritten ms. titled *Retreat II*, p. 35, RSW papers, LPL, MS4134

11 Ward, 'A Little Treatise on Prayer', p. 39, RSW papers, LPL, MS4134

12 *Reginald Somerset Ward 1888 – 1962*, ed. Morgan, pp. 78 – 79

13 Ward, *To Jerusalem*, pp. 7, 8

14 RSW papers, LPL, MS4167

15 On Dorothy Swayne, see: Denise Mumford, *Martha, a life of Dorothy Swayne, lay founder of TSSF* (Third Order of the Society of St Francis, 2014). Swayne's books are *Martha's Prayer Book* (London: SPCK, 1939) reprinted several times and translated into French, and *Martha's Meditation Book* (London: SPCK, 1961)

16 For a discussion of this group, see John Habgood, 'Waiting for God', the Twelfth Eric Symes Abbott lecture (London, The Dean's Office, King's College, London, 1997)

17 A priest [Reginald Somerset Ward], *The Way: devotional studies in mystical religion* (London: Church of England Sunday School Institute, 1922), pp. 12, 7, 8

18 Handwritten notes in RSW's hand; RSW papers, LPL, MS4135, p. 82

19 Ward, *To Jerusalem*, p. 101

20 Reginald Somerset Ward, 'Retreat II, Song of Songs' (unpublished ms., no date) p. 3, RSW papers, LPL, MS3587

21 The Author of *The Way* [Reginald Somerset Ward], *The Experience of God. A Retreat on the Transfiguration* (London: A. R. Mowbray & Co., 1957), pp. 23 – 24

22 Ward, *To Jerusalem*, pp. 186 – 7

23 Ward, *The Way*, pp. 24 – 5, 26, 27

24 Ward, *To Jerusalem*, pp. 17, 21

25 Ward, *To Jerusalem*, p. 18

26 *Reginald Somerset Ward 1881-1962*, ed. Morgan, pp. 81 – 82

27 Underhill, *Collected Papers*, ed. Menzies, pp. 121 – 122, 127

Chapter 3

Percy Dearmer
Beauty

Underhill and Ward were primarily interested in the cultivation of a personal spirituality. Percy Dearmer's interest was rather in public worship, and he was therefore concerned with its decline. 'Can the spirit of public religion be revived?' he asked in those 1919 lectures, published as *The Art of Public Worship*, with which I opened this book.

We ask the question differently today. In the Church of England we talk about the need for discipleship and mission, and in the Episcopal Church in the USA we speak of growing the Episcopal branch of the Jesus movement. But underlying this contemporary language is a basic question that Dearmer, too, was asking a hundred years ago: will Christianity be revived, or at the very least maintained? And underlying that is another question: will more people come to church – and how? Dearmer's answer was: yes, they will, if we make it worth their while through good liturgy. Otherwise, why would anyone bother to go to church? As Dearmer put it, neither a student of Shakespeare nor an ordinary theatre-goer would go to see a play 'where Shakespeare was notoriously murdered by bad declamation, bad music, scenery and costume; he would prefer to read him at home.'[1] So it is with religion.

Percy Dearmer was a priest in the Church of England, described by his biographer, Donald Gray, as 'a hero of faith for our inspiration – and thanksgiving'.[2] His influence has, however, largely been forgotten, even as it continues in numerous ways, from the hymns we sing to the decoration of our churches. Dearmer was born in 1867, which makes him the oldest of our quartet: he was the child of an artist father (who died when he was young) and an unkind mother whom he tolerated patiently. Going to Oxford as an undergraduate, where he read history at Christ Church, was, therefore, a relief and liberation from an unhappy home life. It was also the place where his three intertwined passions came into his life: aesthetics and the arts; liturgy; and social justice.

At Oxford he learned about aestheticism and the arts and crafts movement, reading John Ruskin and hanging William Morris tapestries in his rooms at Christ Church. He came to experience High Church worship and found it closer to his liturgical tastes than the evangelicalism of his mother; and through that discovery he developed a strong interest in English liturgy. Oxford was also the place where he encountered Christian Socialism, getting immediately involved with the Christian Social Union when Henry Scott Holland and Charles Gore founded it in Oxford in 1889, and becoming its secretary until 1912. He also made close friends with whom he went traveling around Europe to see the art he loved, and felt the call to priesthood.

Dearmer was ordained deacon in 1891 and priest in 1892. After ordination he served four curacies, was Vicar of St

Mary's Primrose Hill, served as a chaplain in World War I, was a professor at King's College, London, and finally Canon of Westminster Abbey. His life took him in and out of positions in the Church, and his ministry was as much through his books, teaching and BBC broadcasting as in parish life. The thread that connected everything was his insistence on the centrality of beauty and the sacramental nature of art.

Beauty and the Art of Public Worship

Dearmer believed that worshipping together was an integral part of Christian faith, but it had to be well done. Public worship was, for Dearmer, *always* an art, whether it was good or bad. The artistic components of public worship were the church itself and its decoration; the liturgy; preaching (a rhetorical art); and the music. To make worship breathe and live again, to make it compelling, what lay at the heart of it had to be brought to life – and that was beauty. If public worship was always an art – or composed of several arts – the question was whether it was done in such a way that evoked God's goodness and beauty, and therefore in such a way that enabled the person in the pew to worship God face to face. For beauty has a divine nature, as he declared in his 1924 book, *Art and Religion*. 'Beauty is a quality of God… and art is in fact man's applause to the glory of God.'³

Spirituality, art and beauty were profoundly connected in Dearmer's theology. He wrote: 'Beauty is an eternal quality; it is *found*, whereas art is made: it is the work of God, whereas art is the work of man. Beauty *exists*, and all art is man's [sic] answer to that beauty.' Beauty, like goodness, is a quality of God. Religion and art therefore function in the same way;

51

they are 'manifestations, never fully adequate, of the religious spirit.' They are expressions of the human sense of 'the spiritual significance of the universe.'[4]

Both religion and art are therefore attempts to express that which is unseen and eternal – God and beauty. In that sense, art, like religion, has a sacramental element because beauty, like God, is invisible: both religion and art 'are an attempt to express – not the things which are seen and are temporal, but the things which are unseen and are eternal'.[5] Dearmer radically defined art as sacramental, modifying the traditional understanding of a sacrament by adding beauty to the definition: 'art is a sacrament of the unseen, because it is an outward or visible (or audible) sign of inward spiritual grace *or beauty*' (my italics). It is not surprising, then, that Dearmer rejected any suggestion that art was merely 'an unessential ornament to life which sensible business men can safely ignore'.[6] In a memorable turn of phrase, he wrote against those who believed that 'Art is a frill to the more serious things of life, like the nasty edging of a bishop's sleeves.'[7]

Dearmer was writing at a time when a number of Christian theologians were beginning to think of art as having a redemptive quality, though that was not precisely his angle.[8] Rather, he focused on the transcendent possibilities of art, influenced by his good friend, the essayist and art critic, Arthur Clutton-Brock, who wrote of the ultimate values of Goodness, Truth and Beauty, in his essays on Christianity and art.[9]

Despite appealing to transcendent ideas of beauty, Dearmer's Christian socialism was important in this realm of aesthetics: he believed that art should never be elitist, nor should it be untethered from everyday life; for him art, religion and justice were all connected. As a friend from that time commented, 'Socialism for P.D. meant more than economic change. It meant opening the kingdom of art and beauty to all.' His second wife, Nan, commented: 'Beauty mattered intensely, but it must be shared. If it were not shared it was cold and dead. It was never to be a "frill" on life, but an essential part of living. For him, beauty of worship unallied to the social teachings of the Gospel was sterile; the two were vital to each other and must go hand in hand.'[10] The participation of as many people as possible in the making of art and religion was essential to the health of both. 'The more the people are participants the better it is for art. ... A church whose architecture, carving and painting is owned and shared by all, and where all can help in the singing and take part in the services ... (where, in fact, the service is co-operative and not a sacerdotal affair of the priest or pastor) – such a church is as healthy for art as it is for religion.'[11]

By the time Dearmer was maturing and publishing these thoughts on art, beauty and religion, first in his 1919 Lectures, *The Art of Public Religion*, and then throughout the 1920s, he had had much experience in putting his ideas on art and religion into practice. In 1919, he had been ordained for 28 years, and he had thus far largely devoted his priestly life to practicing the art of public worship. As a curate at churches in London and then – most famously – as Vicar of St Mary's, Primrose Hill, he had put into practice the distinctive liturgical and church aesthetic he had developed as a young man. Based on his experience and his wide reading, he had set out guidelines for how to make worship and church buildings beautiful, and therefore genuinely compelling and appealing, in the book for which he remains most famous, *The Parson's Handbook*, published in 1899 to immediate success. The *Church Times* declared it the most sensible of all the numerous clerical guides that had recently appeared and appealed to its readers to 'help Mr Dearmer on in the good work and not be too proud to acknowledge that we have made mistakes in the past'.[12] The *Handbook's* popularity meant that it went into twelve editions in Dearmer's lifetime and also quickly migrated around the Anglican Communion. It was substantially revised and expanded in 1905, and Oxford University Press published an edition of it as late as 1965.

What was this *Handbook* and why did Dearmer believe it was needed? Dearmer was clear in his Introduction. His *Handbook* was a remedy for the 'lamentable confusion, lawlessness and vulgarity which' he said were 'conspicuous in the Church at this time.' The remedy for this was the Book of Common Prayer, which, he pointed out, all clergy had already sworn to follow. There was 'no excuse' for 'laxity in the conduct of public prayer and the administration of the sacraments'.[13]

What caused such strong words from this earnest 32-year-old (as he was when writing the first edition)? It was not only the sheer variety of styles and practices across the church that caused him concern, but also the adoption of Roman Catholic practices (many of them quite modern in origin) with the rise of High Church practices and ritualism in nineteenth-century Anglicanism.

Dearmer belonged to a group called the Alcuin Club, founded in 1897 with the objective of 'promoting the study of the history and use of the Book of Common Prayer.' Proudly Anglican, its members believed that there was a distinctive 'English Use', which predated the sixteenth-century Reformation, and spoke to continuity in liturgical practice from the medieval church to the present. The Alcuin Club men were Anglo-Catholics; but they were taking a stand against a certain kind of High Church sensibility that looked to Rome rather than England for its ritual style. They objected to six candles on the altar; florid stained glass; and certain practices that the ritualists had introduced, such as not giving communion at the high mass, and the use of Roman Catholic texts in the liturgy. In particular, these 'English Use' Anglo-Catholics were especially obedient to the first prayer book that Thomas Cranmer wrote, the 1549 prayer book, which, they believed, rid the church of the accretions and superstitions of the middle ages, and yet provided continuity, by preserving the native, Catholic traditions of the national English church.

Dearmer and his Alcuin Club friends studied Anglican liturgical history meticulously, and *The Parson's Handbook* had an extraordinary wealth of details about what to wear and in what colours; how to arrange your church; and what to do liturgically. It was in this context that they especially explored the Sarum Rite, developed at Salisbury, the most widely-used of all the medieval liturgical rites.

It was for these reasons, with its appeal to meticulous scholarship made accessible for a wide readership, that Dearmer's *Handbook* was dubbed 'British Museum religion' –

a term first coined by James Adderley, the Christian Socialist priest-in-charge of Berkeley Chapel, John Street, in Mayfair in London, where Dearmer served for a short while as assistant priest. It came later to be used as a jibe or even insult, indicating a kind of pedantic scholarship, but Adderley had not intended it as that. Rather he said that Dearmer 'was just the man to rescue liturgiology from the pedantry of the mere man of letters and make it attractive to the whole Church.'[14]

What was really at the heart of Dearmer's critique was the question of beauty. There had been in the church, he said, a 'neglect of the aesthetic,' even 'vulgarity.'[15] Beauty could bring order to the conduct of worship. D. L. Murray, one of Dearmer's congregants, wrote that Dearmer's 'minute ceremonial research was directed by a large vision, the holiness of beauty serving the beauty of holiness'.[16]

Throughout the *Parson's Handbook*, the aesthetic judgment is therefore paramount: nothing should distract from the simple beauty of worship. Dearmer was opposed to a lot of stained glass because it detracted from the use of colour in altar hangings and vestments. He also brought a sense of style to his analysis; he believed that 'the well-cut surplice is the most beautiful' and 'the use of lace is not an English custom' because 'it simply destroys all beauty of drapery in any garment upon which it is placed.'[17] (This sense of style was also brought to his own everyday garments – not least his Liberty ties.) At the consecration of the elements, during the Eucharist, there should be no incense or lights, in part because the Sarum books did not direct that, but also for aesthetic reasons. He thought that the old spirit of keeping a solemn silence, with nothing to distract the priest, servers or congregation at this supreme moment was the most fitting action.

As for altars, those of 'English Use' were modest, even antiquarian, with a dorsal and riddle curtains (a cloth panel at the back of the altar with curtains at the side) scrupulously avoiding the extravagant and Italianate. As a young man, traveling around Italy, he had written back to friends bemoaning the 'Italian tawdriness'. Attending high mass in the cathedral in Florence he commented on the 'many gorgeous vestments, but an utter absence of any artistic effect whatever' and the 'rotten music'; and he was horrified to discover in one Italian church a set of big candlesticks that were plaster or wood behind and simply silvered in front. This experience informed his passionate advocacy of simple, well-made English design.[18]

Dearmer hoped and even believed that ceremonial uniformity would hold the church together. There was an element of wishful thinking here, and we might well say that Dearmer was inventing a tradition. But he undoubtedly introduced many clergy and laity to the possibility of aesthetic ideals in worship, and the *Handbook*, which went onto so many editions, continued to have an impact well into the middle of the twentieth century and beyond, as the following story of Dearmer's continuing influence illustrates. The late Robert Jeffery, a parish priest in several places, who went on to be Dean of Worcester Cathedral and Sub-Dean of Christ Church Cathedral in Oxford, always gave his curates a copy of Dearmer's *Handbook*. Michael Sadgrove, recently retired as Dean of Durham, worked with Jeffery in Headington, and he relates how Jeffery subtly aided his transformation from the evangelicalism of his youth to English Use Catholicism. 'Without, I think, being aware of it, he [Bob] taught me about "the beauty of holiness" and the genius of the English Church in exemplifying it. He suggested I might like to have a copy of Percy Dearmer's *The Parson's Handbook.*'[19]

In the early twentieth century, Dearmer put his ideas about liturgy and making a worship space as beautiful as possible into practice at St Mary the Virgin, Primrose Hill, where he took up the post of Vicar in 1901. It became an iconic church, exemplifying aesthetic ideals and English Use, demonstrating all the principles that Dearmer expounded in his *Handbook*. D. L. Murray said that Dearmer 'courageously' turned 'an ugly red-brick church' into a 'shrine of beauty, 'with characteristic audacity cutting a gorgeous Bodley reredos in half because, he said, it was out of proportion – and so it was seen to be.'[20] Dearmer limewashed the interior of the whole church, which was red brick and hampered coloured decoration. The colours of the altar hangings and vestments were thus newly highlighted against this light backdrop. He got rid of the Romish six candles on the altar (allegedly one of his first moves) and 'substituted the two candles of English tradition,' and made all the church furnishings conform to English Use principles. As his second wife noted, 'In matters of taste he was completely sure of himself and quite fearless.' He later reflected that maybe he rushed the re-ordering and redecoration of the church, in his youthful enthusiasm.[21]

Dearmer also made the music excellent in innovative and significant ways. In 1903, he and some colleagues had the idea of producing a small book of hymns – intended as a supplement to the eclectic *Hymns Ancient and Modern* which Dearmer attacked, disliking not only its poetical and musical shortcomings, but also the unjust, hierarchical theology it promoted, showing the defects of the age in which it had been created (it had first been published in 1861): 'An age with which we have little in common; the religious world was interested in its own salvation, but was much less interested in God, and not at all in its neighbour – except when he lived a long way off.'[22] Dearmer invited Ralph Vaughan Williams to be the music editor as someone who would understand the wish to create a genuinely *English* Hymnal – the name of the hymn book they produced, described in Dearmer's Preface as 'a collection of the best hymns in the English language'. Many of the hymns were first tried out at St Mary's, Primrose Hill, including 'He who would valiant be' (John Bunyan), 'In the bleak mid-winter' (Christina Rossetti) and 'O God of earth and altar' (G. K. Chesterton), none of which had yet appeared in a hymn book – which seems amazing to us now. The book was published in 1906, and Dearmer had every hope that, like his *Handbook*, the *English Hymnal* would improve artistic standards in church worship. At first, though, it was criticized, not least by several bishops including the Archbishop of Canterbury, for being too high church in its theology, but it eventually went on to be used extensively, especially in cathedrals, and had a great impact.

In his attempts to elevate musical standards in his own church, Dearmer needed a good collaborator. In 1909, through Vaughan Williams, he found the perfect person for his needs – Martin Shaw, who had thus far little to do with church musicians, and much more to do with the theatre. But Shaw had a great interest in English folk music, and it was that expertise in indigenous English music that fitted so perfectly with Dearmer's notion of English Use and broad aesthetic.

Not surprisingly, the church attracted artists, writers and social reformers from all parts of London. Peter Anson, a writer on religious and architectural themes who went on to become a monk, slightly tongue-in-cheek said that the younger members of the congregation were almost certainly to be Christian Socialists and vegetarian, with an urge to live in garden cities, or quaint little houses.[23] In that sense, St Mary's Primrose Hill became something of a gathered church, where people chose to go because of what was going on, and not necessarily because it was their parish. Maude Royden, later the well-known preacher and activist for the ordination of women, was one of those parishioners. She wrote that, when she first went to live in London, after wandering about to different churches, she went to St Mary's, Primrose Hill, to see if she liked the services there. 'I did like them; I felt immediately and utterly at home and never strayed away until Percy Dearmer gave up his ministry in the war.'[24] D. L. Murray wrote that he was drawn to the church because, as 'an ecclesiological schoolboy,' he had been 'bitten by the fascination of ritualistic study ... and "Dearmerism" had been reported to me as a special brand.'[25]

With his artist wife Mabel, Dearmer created a deeply artistic house, a homage to the arts and crafts movement, where beauty was taken with the utmost seriousness. When they moved in to the new vicarage in 1907, for example, everything was up-to-date in the arts and crafts fashion. The drawing room had cream wallpaper with nine tall rose-trees blossoming on it; there were chairs of rose-coloured chintz, and a grass-green carpet.[26] Furniture and crockery were all handmade. Mabel and Percy Dearmer were putting into practice their shared belief in good design, buying objects, furnishings and furniture made in workshops or by individual craftspeople rather than that which was industrially-created and mass-produced.

None of this should be taken as art for art's sake, though as an undergraduate at Oxford Dearmer had read Walter Pater's late nineteenth-century work which advocated that idea. Rather, for Dearmer, it was art for God's sake and art for justice. The relationship between God, beauty and justice was worked out in his concern for the decline in art, how things were made, and the working conditions of those who made them. In the introduction to the first edition of *The Parson's Handbook*, he wrote 'It has been pointed out that a modern preacher often stands in a sweated pulpit, wearing a sweated surplice over a suit of clothes that were not produced under fair conditions, and, holding a sweated book in one hand, with the other he points to the machine-made cross at the jerry-built altar, and appeals to the sacred principles of mutual sacrifice and love.' Vulgarity – against which he railed in the *Handbook* – was related to cheapness, which was related to the use of sweated labour.[27] Here Dearmer was again revealing the twin influences of the arts and crafts movement and Christian Socialism, opposing machine manufacturing and unfair (sweated) labour practices.

61

Concern about both aesthetics and working conditions led him first to form the St Dunstan's Society in 1901, to make surplices, albs, hoods and vestments according to approved patterns, and secondly, in 1912, the Warham Guild. This was established in cooperation with Mowbray's, to make and sell ornaments and vestments of the type he recommended in the *Handbook*, with the assurance that those items were made under good and fair working conditions.

On the Fringes of the Church

We opened our exploration of Dearmer in 1919, with his work *The Art of Public Religion*. At that point, he was recovering from the horrors of World War I. The war had been personally traumatic for Dearmer, and marked a turning point for him. In March 1915, he had been so moved by reports of what was happening in Serbia that he decided to go as a chaplain to the British units working in that country. With both of their sons at the Front, his wife Mabel had decided she too should go to Serbia to nurse in one of the field hospitals there. They went together, and six months later, in July, Mabel died of a fever she caught there. Dearmer returned to England and, just a few months later, in October, news came that his son Christopher had been killed by a stray shell that fell onto his tent. Dearmer was by then back working at St Mary's Primrose Hill, but life could not go back to normal. Since 1910, he had been hoping for the offer of another job in the Church, but none was forthcoming. He resigned from St Mary's, went to work in France and then accepted an invitation to work in India as a missionary for a year, leaving in the autumn of 1916 after marrying his second wife Nan, whom he had known for many years. (William Temple married them at St James's, Piccadilly, where Temple was then Rector.)

From 1916, when he resigned his Primrose Hill living, to 1931, Dearmer held no position in the Church, nor was he offered one. Those fifteen years on the margins of the church were difficult – he wanted to be offered a position – but doubtless they enabled him to understand the institutional church better, and its lack of appeal to people especially in the wake of World War I.

From India, he and Nan went to America, where he was invited to teach at Berkeley Divinity School, an Episcopal Seminary in Connecticut, for a period. There he taught liturgy and theology, and gave the Page Lectures on the Power of the Spirit, and, characteristically, designed the altar and altar hangings for the seminary's temporary chapel. He enjoyed learning first-hand about the American Book of Common Prayer and using it in worship both at the seminary and in the many churches he visited as a guest preacher. It was also while he was there that he travelled to Philadelphia to deliver the Boehling Lectures on the Art of Public Worship. Nan and Percy Dearmer returned to England in 1919 where he took up the newly created position of Professor of Church Art at King's College, London, which had been largely created for him, with a salary of a mere hundred pounds.

Holding no job within the Church of England, Dearmer took the opportunity to work with those whom he had discussed in his 1919 Lectures: 'those who no longer attended that which they do not like.' In 1920, he suggested to Maude Royden, who had worshipped at St Mary's Primrose Hill, that she might form a place of her own. By this time, she – an Anglican – had a calling to public ministry, but the Church of England ignored it (indeed, forbade her to preach), so she was working at the City Temple, a Congregationalist church in London, which had allowed her to preach. However, with the advent of a new minister there, she foresaw that she might not be able to remain, and so she agreed to Dearmer's suggestion – as long as he helped her. Royden shared Dearmer's commitment to building a better society, to beauty and its place in public worship (she had after all been shaped by worshipping at Primrose Hill) and to reaching those outside the church.

The Guild of Fellowship, as they named their group, began as a non-denominational worshipping community in 1920, holding fellowship services in Kensington Town Hall, but when the numbers reached 1000, in 1921, The Guildhouse was founded and met in a former Congregationalist chapel in Eccleston Square near Victoria Station in London (until 1936, when it moved to Bloomsbury, and then dissolved just before the outbreak of the war).

At the very first service they held, they made a statement about their purpose (this was on March 21st, 1920):

> Our feeling is that the Church of England, like other Churches in this country, is at present appealing to that minority of English people who go to church on Sunday – a minority which appears to be decreasing. She ought to appeal to the public at large, by means of addresses and informal gatherings for discussion, and to speak to the great body of people who are not at home in church,

or who do not even know their way about the Prayer-Book. Very probably there should be a centre of this sort in every district of our great cities, and certainly several in London.

Among students and the younger generation especially, there is a large number – and those often amongst the ablest and most religious – who are estranged from 'organized religion,' who have, as they say, 'no use' for churches.

The effects in the next twenty years will be serious, unless some people make efforts to help those who are not attracted by the methods of the parish church.[28]

The message still sounds familiar. The Guildhouse might well qualify today for Fresh Expressions funding, 'to start a church with people who do not go to church' as the USA and UK Fresh Expressions movement describes its goals.[29]

Royden and Dearmer were clear, however, that they did not intend The Guildhouse to be a new church or a schismatic sect. They held services, meetings and study groups on Sunday and weekday *evenings*, in order not to clash with Sunday morning services, and they did not celebrate Communion. But Royden did say in 1920, 'if those of us who desire reform are all forced to leave our own churches we shall found another church. People who desire any great reform must create a fellowship in which to work for it.'[30] Royden was by now a much-celebrated preacher and leader of worship, with a clearly expressed vocation to ordained ministry, but she was forbidden from preaching or participating in any leadership functions in the Church of England.

Dearmer and Royden saw that they could try out things that were not always possible in a parish church. 'There is also a crying need for experiments at the present time in the creation of a more vivid sense of fellowship among Christian people; in the services which may be rendered by the laity; and by women, who have been less valued by the Churches than laymen; in the revision of the Prayer Book, and many other directions.'[31]

The Sunday afternoon service was devised by Dearmer, and called Five Quarters (because it lasted an hour and a quarter). It regularly attracted 500 people, and topics for discussion ranged from world religions to science and society to the arts to Gandhi and the peace movement. The actress Peggy Ashcroft read modern poetry there and Gilbert Murray, the classicist, recited Euripides, while prominent politicians would come to discuss the pressing political issues of the day. Alongside these talks and recitations were readings from the Bible and music – hymns, canons, motets, orchestral pieces and solos. The 6:30 service (which followed the Five Quarters) was when Royden preached or, in her absence, Dearmer. (She went on some extensive preaching tours around the world throughout the 1920s.)

The aesthetic was, of course, important. Dearmer took charge of the re-decoration of the chapel, a building which Royden feared, at first sight, was too ugly. He whitewashed the walls, and highlighted vibrant colours against that backdrop: blue cassocks for stewards; red music books for all; beautiful pulpit cushions and lanterns. The Guildhouse was also a laboratory for the arts in worship: 'We desire, further, to bring into the service of religion all that is lovely in music and the other arts, and we especially hope – since we belong to the Church of England – to develop the church music of our own country, which was once the peculiar gift of the English Church.'[32] To that end, Dearmer brought his old friend Martin Shaw along to be Master of music.

The Guildhouse provided multiple avenues and media (art, science, literature, various religious traditions) by which the divine might be revealed to a crowd that was often 'spiritual but not religious.' The Guildhouse was composed mostly of women and young working people. It appealed to those who were dissatisfied with ordinary church; those who were idealistic – 'We take for our principle the pursuit of "the good, the beautiful and the true"'[33] declared the Guildhouse early on; those who wanted to learn; and those who were lonely and found community there. Women were especially attracted to the Guildhouse because it gave them work and roles in leading worship, social action and teaching (in other words, responsibility *with* authority). The Guildhouse had the particular appeal of Royden's preaching, which addressed the real problems of post-war society, but in an optimistic, we-can-fix-this way that many found heartening and encouraging. It was appealing especially to middle class and lower middle-class single, independent women, such as teachers and secretaries, who had perhaps moved to London alone, providing them with fellowship. Percy Dearmer's second wife, Nan, in her biography of him, regarded this aspect of The Guildhouse as something of a failure, while so much else was a success. Nan Dearmer wrote: 'The Guildhouse was packed each

Sunday night when Miss Royden was preaching, but it was packed almost entirely by women, very few men joined the congregation. This was unfortunate, as it gave a pronounced feminist atmosphere to the place and restricted its influence in a way that had not been foreseen.'[34] This seems to have been very much Nan Dearmer's perspective, rather than that of either Percy Dearmer or Maude Royden.

For Dearmer, women's suffrage had been a cause he cared about and had shared with his first wife Mabel; the ordination of women was an issue of justice within the church, and he was one of the first people to take it up and may even have influenced Royden in this. Back in 1913, a radical Anglican vicar's wife named Ursula Roberts had written to several of her liberal contacts in the church suggesting that they have a meeting about the question of ordaining women in the Church of England. Some people were cautiously interested, including Maude Royden, but it was Dearmer who really grasped the idea initially and offered his church in Primrose Hill for the meeting.[35] War broke out in 1914, and the meeting was deferred for several years. In the meantime, Royden began preaching regularly, and took on the mantle of chief campaigner, but Percy Dearmer's support should not be underestimated. He would have been pleased that his granddaughter, Juliet Woollcombe, is a priest. Dearmer and Royden shared a passion for justice and equity, and made the main areas of reform the ministry of women; the ministry of laypeople; and work for peace.

The Guildhouse took up many causes and activities. On weekdays, it was buzzing with its multiplicity of clubs and events. On Mondays Boy Scouts, the Women Citizens group and the law clinic; Tuesdays The Guildhouse Players (a dramatic society) and a branch of the League of Nations Union; Wednesdays the Girl Guides; Thursdays a special prayer service, and so on. The League of Arts, founded in 1918 and given an office at the Guildhouse, was very active in producing plays and pageants, usually performed in Hyde Park. Historian Alison Falby portrays The Guildhouse as successful because it found a new language for old ideas.[36]

In 1924, Dearmer left The Guildhouse, feeling that it was up and running, and he should turn to other things. He was teaching at King's College, London, but was still not offered another position in the Church. Nan Dearmer wrote that 'the unattached years ... were a trial for Percy; he could not but feel that his gifts were unappreciated.' She described him as 'pre-eminently an originator of new ideas, and to such a man reward rarely comes in a lifetime.' She remarks: 'at times he spoke with acidity of his treatment, but he avoided the obvious danger of becoming conditioned by bitterness.'[37] Many people thought he should have been made a cathedral dean for his obvious interests in liturgy and the arts, his vision and capacity to execute new ideas, his desire to embrace those outside institutional religion – all this would have made him an excellent dean. Instead, in 1931, he was appointed a Canon of Westminster Abbey, where he worked until his death aged 69 in 1936, having been a popular preacher, and a major contributor to the work of the Abbey's Library, and organizer of a canteen for the unemployed based at the abbey.

Dearmer's work was important both inside and outside the church. He sat lightly to the institution and was able therefore to see its strengths and weaknesses with clarity. His friends came from many different areas of life, and included the artists and suffragettes whom he met through Mabel, his first wife; musicians with whom he collaborated on multiple projects; his old college friends; those with whom he worked when he was broadcasting children's programmes through the BBC and those with whom he produced plays and pageants for wide audiences in London; and Christian socialist companions on the path of justice. In this sense, he never became too 'churchy' or too locked into 'institutional-think.' He therefore had a capacious sense of the church's reach into and *reliance upon* all areas of life; he certainly did not think that the church had all the answers. Most of all he articulated in his writings and demonstrated through liturgy, the arts and his political engagement the connections between God, justice and beauty.

These were all ideals and themes that had significance for our fourth spiritual pioneer, Rose Macaulay.

Notes

1   Dearmer, *The Art of Public Worship*, pp. 6 – 7

2   Donald Gray, *Percy Dearmer: A Parson's Pilgrimage* (Norwich: Canterbury Press, 2000), p. 5

3   Dearmer, *Art and Religion* (London: SCM Press, 1924), p. 16

4   Dearmer, *Art and Religion*, pp. 15 – 16

5   Dearmer, *Art and Religion*, p. 16

6   Dearmer, *Art and Religion*, pp. 11 – 12, 4, 2

7   Dearmer, *The Art of Public Worship*, p. 13

8   See Frances Knight, *Victorian Christianity at the Fin-de-Siecle: The Culture of English Religion in a Decadent Age* (London: I. B. Tauris, 2016), chapter 9

9   See, for example, A. Clutton-Brock, *The Ultimate Belief* (London: Constable and Co., New York: E.P. Dutton and Co., 1916) and *Studies in Christianity* (London: Constable and Co., 1918). Nan Dearmer wrote of the late 1910s and early 1920s that 'Percy was more influenced by Arthur Brock than by anyone else at this period, and much that Arthur said and wrote became part of his own teaching. Almost too much so, for he preached the Ultimate Value of Goodness, Truth and Beauty, in and out of season, until some of his hearers longed for a change of theme.' Nan Dearmer, *The Life of Percy Dearmer* (London: The Book Club, 1941), p. 228

10 Nan Dearmer, *The Life*, pp. 35, 35 – 36.

11 Dearmer, *Art and Religion*, p. 17

12 Quoted in Gray, *Percy Dearmer*, p. 45

13 Percy Dearmer, *The Parson's Handbook* (London: Grant Richards, 1899 [1st edition]), pp. 1, 6

14 Quoted in Nan Dearmer, *The Life*, p. 104

15 Percy Dearmer, *The Parson's Handbook* (London: Oxford, University Press, 1932 [12th edition]), p 4; Percy Dearmer, *The Parson's Handbook* [1st edition], p. 3

16 Quoted in Nan Dearmer, *The Life*, p. 138

17 Dearmer, *Parson's Handbook* [12th edition], p. 128

18 Nan Dearmer, *The Life*, p. 49

19 Michael Sadgrove, 'In Memoriam: Bob Jeffery, Priest, Mentor, Friend', 23 February, 2017, at http://northernwoolgatherer.blogspot.com

20 Quoted in Nan Dearmer, *The Life*, p. 137

21 Nan Dearmer, *The Life*, p. 117

22 Quoted in Gray, *Percy Dearmer*, p. 62

23 Quoted in Gray, *Percy Dearmer*, p. 72

24 Quoted in Nan Dearmer, *The Life*, pp. 240 – 241

25 Quoted in Nan Dearmer, *The Life*, p. 137

26 Nan Dearmer, *The Life*, p. 151

27 Dearmer, *The Parson's Handbook* [1st edition], p. 5

28 Quoted in Nan Dearmer, *A Life*, pp. 245 – 6

29 This is a movement in both the USA and UK. See, for example, https://www.churchofengland.org/our-faith/mission/missionevangelism/fresh-expressions.aspx and http://freshexpressionsus.org

30 Quoted in Alison Falby, 'Maude Royden's Guildhouse: A Nexus of Religious Change in Britain between the Wars' in *Historical Papers 2004: Canadian Society of Church History*, p. 3

31 Quoted in Nan Dearmer, *A Life*, p. 246

32 Nan Dearmer, *A Life*, p. 247

33 Quoted in Sheila Fletcher, *Maude Royden, A Life* (Oxford: Basil Blackwell,1989), p. 215

34 Nan Dearmer, *A Life*, p. 248

35 Percy Dearmer to Ursula Roberts, 2nd December 1913; Percy Dearmer to Ursula Roberts, 27th June, 1914; Stanford University Libraries (Manuscript Division), M0908

36 See Falby, 'Maude Royden's Guildhouse'; Falby gives details about the many activities at the Guildhouse, and their appeal.

37 Nan Dearmer, *A Life*, p. 268

Chapter 4

Rose Macaulay
Second Chances

In 1950, Rose Macaulay, then living in London, received an airmail letter from one John Hamilton Cowper Johnson of 980 Memorial Drive, Cambridge, Massachusetts, better known as Father Johnson of the Society of St John the Evangelist (SSJE). He was writing because he had enjoyed her most recent novel, *They Were Defeated*. It was a fan letter from a monk. Macaulay replied, and so began a correspondence that lasted for eight years, until her death, and changed Macaulay's life.

Father Johnson had met Rose Macaulay some thirty years earlier when he had been at St Edward's House, the SSJE monastic house in Westminster, when he had been leading a retreat that she was on. But when their lively correspondence began in 1950, Macaulay had been out of the church of her youth, the Church of England, for nearly thirty years. She had been in a long relationship with a married man and had not known how to reconcile that with her faith. In 1950, that man had been dead for several years; Father Johnson's epistolary entry into Macaulay's life was timely.

Who was Rose Macaulay? We might begin with her own words from the end of her life. These are the things she told her sister Jean that she would say about herself on the BBC's *Women's Hour* in 1958, after she had been awarded a DBE, and a few months before she died:

> I think they said they would ask me about things I like and don't like. If so, I shall probably say I like beautiful country and buildings, driving through romantic scenery, swimming in warm seas when no one else is doing so near me, good company and talk, listening to good music, including a very well sung and orchestrated Mass. ... I shall say I dislike crooning, especially vulgar and silly love songs, repairing things that have gone wrong, such as my car, my clothes etc., religious intolerance (I don't mind other intolerance nearly so much, as it isn't paradoxical), industrial towns, ugly and monotonous rows of houses, etc. ... The more vulgar and silly newspapers I might add.[1]

Here is some more straightforward biography. She was born in 1881, the same year as Reginald Somerset Ward; she was therefore six years younger than Evelyn Underhill and fourteen years younger than Percy Dearmer. She grew up in an academic family, in Italy as a young girl and then, from the age of 13, in Oxford, where she attended Oxford High School for Girls and then Somerville College, Oxford, where she read history and developed her great passion for the seventeenth century. After that she went to live in Aberystwyth where her father had gone to teach, and she began writing novels, and then moved with her family to Great Shelford, a village outside

Cambridge – where her father was, from 1906, teaching at Cambridge University. Then a move to London gave her greater freedom and friendship with an ever-widening circle of writers that included Virginia Woolf, E. M. Forster, Vita Sackville-West and Harold Nicholson, Gilbert Murray and others. At the end of World War I, she met and fell in love with Gerald O'Donovan, a former Jesuit priest who was already married with children. They developed a close relationship, meeting frequently in London and enjoying annual holidays together, until his death in 1942. During these years she became well known as a writer, mostly of novels, but also of non-fiction, including essays on historical themes and travel, and some poetry. The Second World War was a devastating time for Macaulay, not only for the death of O'Donovan, but also for the death of a sister Margaret, who was a deaconess, and because her flat was bombed and she lost most of her belongings, including all her books and unpublished manuscripts. She also became very ill. She bounced back after the war and began writing again. But when that fan letter arrived from Father Johnson, she was potentially receptive to what he had to offer.

This chapter is about Rose Macaulay's return to faith at the age of 69 and it is therefore about second chances. But it is also about a great theme of the twentieth century, for Rose Macaulay represents all those who had doubt, who wanted to know *how we know*, who had questions about the faith and yet remained fascinated by it while on the margins or outside it. So this chapter is also about her lifelong fascination with religion, despite those decades outside the church – the 1920s, 30s and 40s – when she described herself as Anglo-agnostic.

My focus is not on her novels, but on her correspondence with Father Johnson and with her sister Jean, a district nurse, who was always a devout Anglican. Rose Macaulay's letters to Father Johnson are full of learning, wit, charm and most of all deep questions about faith. And two other – related – things are of interest for the themes of this book: her rootedness in Anglicanism, despite absence from the Church; and the ways in which she conceives of seeing God through 'frames.' Her letters to her sister are charming, funny, full of what she was doing, religion, gossipy and sometimes indiscreet. In fact, when her sister Jean first went through the letters, after Rose's death, she destroyed the most scurrilous ones, so what we have is not a complete set.

It is my contention that Rose Macaulay returned to faith not just because her soul was ready, though that was a large part of it; not just because she entered into a correspondence with the right monk at the right time, though that was also part of it; but because she was steeped in the history and culture of Anglicanism, and she could draw on this – what she called her spiritual capital. For Macaulay, this was so much the case that she felt that she could be nothing but Anglican, and loved the liturgy, art and literature that were at the heart of the Church of England. She had a very profound understanding of the ways in which we know God not directly but through 'frames' as she put it, and for her those frames were in particular the liturgy and music she found in church. In fact, she found it difficult to perceive of being a Quaker, for example, because she felt they 'make a mistake, in having no frame, only direct communications.'[2]

She grew up in a devout Anglican family, and was confirmed at the Church of St Philip and St James (known as Pip and Jim) in Oxford when she was 14 years old. She later admitted that she already had religious doubts at the time but did not feel able to raise them. There is no sign that she was seriously religious for some time until – much to the whole family's shock – her brother was murdered in 1909 while working in the Royal Engineers in India. Rose's initial response was to offer herself, rather impulsively, as a missionary in central Africa; she was turned down as unsuitable and knew better than to ever offer herself for this kind of work again. Instead, she sought to deepen her faith and went on a retreat with her mother and sister at St Alban's Holborn; it was around this time that she became avowedly Anglo-Catholic in her sensibilities. She also met Father Waggett, a Cowley Father (SSJE), well-known as a preacher. This meant that when she moved to London, she immediately associated herself with St Edward's House in Westminster, which was the SSJE headquarters in London, making her confession there – sometimes to a young Father Johnson, for this is where they first met.

He noted, later, that they met about half a dozen times in London where they had little conversation beyond her confession, though she also joined a Retreat for Women (or perhaps it was called a Retreat for Ladies, he later wondered!) that he conducted somewhere in a convent in the suburbs. There he remembered looking out of the window 'into the little, dull, square garden, and seeing Miss Macaulay pacing up and down very gravely and slowly. I think on the grass, for a long while, in steadily drizzling rain, tall and grave and thoughtful, wearing some sort of dark tweed suit – no overcoat or raincoat. This she did for a long time.'[3] Soon after that, in 1916, Father Johnson left for the American SSJE house, in Cambridge, Massachusetts. And, in 1918, Macaulay met Gerald O'Donovan, and began to slip away from the church, unable to reconcile her relationship with her faith, deciding in 1922 that she could no longer receive communion or make her confession.

She still went to church from time to time – for example, in 1926 she went to the Good Friday service at Grosvenor Chapel where she heard Francis Underhill speak (whom she mistakenly thought was the cousin of Evelyn Underhill) but her attendance dwindled even as an interest in liturgy and church gossip remained. Her sister Jean separated out Rose's interest in the *form* of religion from religion itself, 'much as a conductor of an orchestra may be interested in every detail of the production while realising the essential thing is the music. Rose and I used to discuss at length every detail of Church Services, in the years when she cut herself off from religion, as well as after.'[4]

In those decades away from the Church, she therefore never lost some sense of engagement with and interest in the Church, even when she was not attending services, as her letters to her sister Jean attest. She continued to have friends who were priests and loved conversations with them. Here is her description, to her sister, of a conversation over tea, after a visit to the cinema with a priest friend, J. K. (Kenneth)

Mozley, as he explained that 'he was the only true Augustinian in the Church, much to the amusement of the neighbouring tea tables. "'I have no use at all, my dear Rose," he said, getting very loud and shrill, "for your weak, striving, well-meaning God, who has to rely on our encouragement of him for his success." Everyone looked at me with scorn, for having a God like that. I like to see a man so animated about religion.' (Mozley was an Anglo-Catholic who also appreciated the work of Karl Barth.) She later commented that Mozley, a canon of St Paul's cathedral, had a medieval mind and had been born 600 years too late. She became especially friendly in the 1930s with Dick Sheppard, from St Martin's in the Fields, for they shared a deep commitment to pacifism. She wrote in 1936 to her sister Jean 'You would like him very much, he is so friendly and enthusiastic and he has such a live idea of Christianity.'[5]

She was always opinionated about the clergy and their engagement, or lack of it, with the world. She sent an article to her sister about an actress recommending 'all women to spend their money on beauty improvement. What can we do about this? I am writing an article, and I think we should all SPEAK about it, it is too degraded and fearful. With all those … unsupported hospitals and penniless old people – and this woman says she would rather go hungry than be plain – and what she means is she would rather other people went hungry than she were plain. Sometimes I wish I were a clergyman, a bishop, a pope, or a dean, to speak out from a pulpit. When the clergy do preach on beauty culture, they do it all wrong saying it is ungodly and immodest, instead of attacking its selfishness and imbecility.'[6] She continued to be opinionated about the clergy – writing in her very first letter to Father Johnson in 1950: 'I rather wish the rising generations of clergy were more intellectual; so many seem rather chumps; or do I generalize from inadequate experience.'[7] And indeed many of the cuts that Constance Babington Smith made to the published letters to Father Johnson were indiscreet comments Macaulay made about clergy who were still living at the time that the letters were published.

During her years outside the church, she still keenly followed church debates in the national newspapers but also in the *Church Times*, and she read with approval many of W. R. Inge's articles in the *Evening Standard* (the Dean of St Paul's Cathedral, whom we encountered briefly in Chapter One, as one of the main revivers of mysticism in the early twentieth century). She continued to read books about Anglicanism and other religious matters, and recommended them to her sister.

She also rescued religious books, as the novelist A. N. Wilson relates in a moving anecdote about the morning after the London Library – where she spent so much time reading and exploring the bookshelves – had been bombed in 1942. Wilson writes, 'One member is alleged to have emerged from the burnt out stacks on the top floor and said … "We've lost our Religion".' He continues: 'Higher up than the lost religion, staff and members were struggling to save as many books as possible from the wreckage. A tangle of girders stretched out like tormented fingers to the open sky. Everything was covered with grey dust, and shelves of books, apparently suspended on air, dangled precariously in the sky, in imminent danger of being wrecked by rain, having been spared by fire.

… Rose Macaulay was the bravest, telling them to hang on to her legs as she leant out into space.'[8]

So, when she began a correspondence with Father Johnson in 1950, she had a bedrock of knowledge and certainly plenty of opinions about the Church of England, and Christianity more generally, upon which to build. Early on, she wrote in answer to a comment of his:

> Yes, I supposed I *am* grounded in religious knowledge more or less, having been brought up that way; and, also, perhaps, inheriting an interest in theology and church literature from a thousand (or so) clerical ancestors who, I presume, had it all at their fingertips. Of late years, I'm afraid it has got rather rusty; but I do still know days and psalms and creeds and even most of the major heresies.[9]

In Father Johnson, she found a perfect conversation partner for her learning and religious interests. He was a bookish monk and Anglo-Catholic priest who loved Latin and liturgy, with a reputation, amongst his brothers at the monastery and those to whom he ministered, for compassion and kindness in spiritual direction and as a confessor and pastor.

John Hamilton Cowper Johnson – known as Hamilton – was born in 1877, four years before Macaulay, and he was the son of a Church of England rector in Norfolk. He read Classics at New College, Oxford, and then went to Cuddesdon College, just outside Oxford, to train for the ordained ministry, being ordained deacon in 1903 and priest in 1904. In 1906 he joined the Society of St John the Evangelist in Cowley, Oxford (the place where the order was founded); from there he went to St Edward's House in London, from 1914 to 1916 (which is where Macaulay met him) before going out to join the American branch of the order, where he stayed until his death in 1961. That transfer was in part the result of his feeling in disgrace for an innocent but misguided relationship with an invalid young woman in London, of which his Superior in England disapproved. Father Powell, Superior of the SSJE house in Cambridge, Massachusetts, was visiting at the time and invited him to America. In this small way, Father Johnson experienced a second chance, and he knew how to offer that generosity of second chances to others.

For much of his time in America (until the 1940s) he was based not at the monastery in Cambridge, but at the Mission church that the order ran in Boston: St John the Evangelist. There he greeted people, ministered to them and gently brought them to faith, including two circus performer sisters who wished to be baptized but had been rejected by the Baptist church (where they went first) which had tried to insist that, if baptized, they give up their acrobatic profession. Somehow, they found their way to Father Johnson at the church in Boston where he baptized them, and thereafter stayed in touch with them as they went on their itinerant way, suggesting churches where they might worship while on their circus tours. He did not preach much, however, because the Superior did not think he was up to it, as he had a hesitating manner of speech. Father David Allen, SSJE, suggests however, that this was not because of nervousness but because he was looking for the right word. In fact he had a beautiful voice, and the monks enjoyed him reading to them during meals; it had been even more beautiful in his youth – a deep bass with great resonance – but he had apparently one day demonstrated some Maltese folksongs, from his time of living in Malta as a young man, and his voice was never the same again.[10]

Father Johnson's precision in wordsmithing made him a perfect correspondent for someone such as Rose Macaulay. What may have been less than compelling in the pulpit was attractive in epistolary form. Because Macaulay's and Father Johnson's conversation took place through correspondence, both could manage the pace of it, choosing their words carefully. And it is clear – even though we do not have Father Johnson's letters – that they both relished this opportunity to bring so much of their lives to this correspondence, very quickly important to them both. It is worth evoking one of Father Johnson's (few) sermons here. Preaching on Philippians 3:20 – 'Our conversation is in heaven' – in the Church of St John the Evangelist in Boston in 1941, he expounded upon the meaning of conversation, turning for illumination to the Latin word 'conversatio' – meaning, he translated, 'a whole way of life, and of interests, rather than merely talking with one another.' Certainly, the correspondence between him and Rose Macaulay was about 'a whole way of life, and of interests' if Macaulay's letters are an accurate indicator.[11]

The correspondence began in August 1950, but quite quickly, Macaulay began to write with both feeling and depth about her departure from faith. In her first letter to him, she wrote that it was many years since she had been to a retreat or anything of that nature, and 'I have sadly lost touch with that side of life, and regret it.' She went on, 'We do need it so badly, in this queer world and life, all going to pieces and losing.' She was acutely aware of the decline of religion and believed that had particular repercussions. 'Many of my younger friends have never had it and haven't, therefore, the ultimate sanction for goodness, unselfishness, integrity, kindness, self-denial, which those brought up to believe in God accept at any rate as ideals, even if they have lost their belief.'[12] As her correspondence with Father Johnson continued about their mutual religious and literary interests, her longing to believe emerged, so that by the end of October, only two months after the correspondence began, she wrote:

> I like to pick up and follow your trails in hope. … What, too sadly likely, I may not pick up, is the power to believe these things – I mean the actual facts (as you put it, what God has done). How I wish I could get there. Partly my difficulties are intellectual – I just can't make the grade – partly, I sometimes think, the blindness that comes from the selfish and deplorable life I've led. Who knows? It's all a kind of vicious circle – badness keeps one from the realisation of God, perhaps nothing but that could cure badness … And I expect one has to find a way through by some other road, that one can more easily accept.[13]

She had long been a doubter, and the question of *knowing* and how we know God still haunted her: 'That question about knowing. I have often asked it of believing friends and relations. They say it depends on what you mean by 'know'. They *feel* certain. Or, in some cases are putting their shirts on a *hope*, because if it's not true, they feel they might as well lose the shirt along with everything else of value to them – they are quite right, of course. I wish I had as much guts.' But she appreciated the correspondence with Father Johnson, 'a wonderful *revenance* from the far past, which I never supposed would cross my orbit again. It gives me a lot to consider.'[14]

She was, soon, to have enough guts, largely because of Father Johnson's delicate kindness. We do not, alas, have his letters to her as Macaulay instructed that all her papers in her flat at her death be destroyed (and they were, by her sister Jean) but she had written to him about the relationship she had had with a married man and he clearly replied with enormous sympathy and acceptance. By mid-December she was writing to thank him for 'being so immeasurably wise, good and understanding.' Again, the text of a sermon is helpful in the absence of his letters: this time, a sermon he preached on the Pharisee and the Publican (Luke 18:9 – 14) reveals something of his attitude, how much he disliked judgmental or self-righteous Christians, and how generous in outlook he was. He asked his congregation:

> Are any of us, perhaps, among those who have sometimes felt rather pleased to be able to feel a certain amount of rather pleasant, and even religious satisfaction, in our own sense of self-satisfaction, in the thought that, by our own efforts or excellence of character, we have succeeded in being pretty good sort of people? Have we even derived some additional satisfaction from the thought that others, perhaps, whom we know from 'A to Z' have by no means managed to make such a good showing? If so, we are just the people to whom our Lord is now desiring to speak.[15]

Father Johnson's non-judgmental kindness enabled Macaulay to reveal many of her inner thoughts to him; to unburden herself. She was entirely comfortable with the epistolary confession to him as this remarkable passage, about what it was like to live in those years away from the church, reveals, with its two contrasting metaphors of a treacle well and a blank wall.

> I suppose I ... have lived in ... a treacle well ... a climate of opinion and attitude in which the people one knows – and often likes or loves – do that kind of thing often, and don't think badly of it in themselves or others. So gradually, if one is doing it oneself, one sinks more and more well in, and can't even see clearly what it really is. One gets clogged about; treacle is so clinging. No doubt I am still partly in; though it is over, one can't struggle right out. To change the metaphor, long years of wrong-doing build a kind of blank – or nearly blank – wall between oneself and God, and the task is to break it down, or at least make holes in it large enough to see through. It isn't, of course, God who puts up the wall; it is one's own actions and rejections.[16]

Father Johnson was gently suggesting she might make her confession to a priest in London, and in response to that she wrote: 'As to absolution, I suppose this would make holes in the wall. Absolution from Memorial Drive [the address of SSJE in Cambridge], which I feel I have (however undeservedly), has already made some.' She wondered how she might compress 30 years into a confession – 'I suppose it will get done somehow. I wish you were here.' When she finally did so, going to one of the SSJE priests, Father Wilkins in London, at Father Johnson's suggestion, the experience left her 'winded and dazed' and surprised that Father Wilkins said practically nothing to her except the absolution. She was grateful for Father Johnson, 'her non-resident chaplain' to whom she could ask all her questions, and who was not afraid to offer advice. 'Thank God, you give this; if you didn't I should still be sticking in the wrong treacle well like a fly.' And one feels all her passion and longing for God in this question, humorously put, but so heartfelt:

> dear non-resident chaplain, I would like to ask you, were it not so formidably vast a question how people vitiated and weakened by a long course of knowingly wrong living, can become strong, intelligent, and moderately good. It really is a question. But I suppose I know the main answer, really.

Just four months into the correspondence, she wrote to Father Johnson:

> How many people do you 'change' a year, I wonder? I expect, a lot. Beginning with talk about things in general, sacred and profane, and largely in a profane language; sacred things coming in more as time goes on; fresh light on all kinds of topics, 'a rising and a growing light' as Donne says, and a stirring of the conscience – till, before one knows where one is, one is surrendering to a new (or old) way of life and wanting to lead it. And all in about 4 months![17]

Father Johnson gave her spiritual wisdom from the distance of 3000 miles, soon guiding her to priests and churches in London. Macaulay's taste remained decidedly High Church, and she would get into her little car, which she drove with alarming recklessness, and head to one of the Anglo-Catholic churches within a five-mile radius of her Hinde Street flat, for Mass. Sometimes it was All Saints, Margaret Street, for 'a magnificent service,' but she really preferred 'the more quiet style of Grosvenor Chapel; no crowds, no choir; incense yes, and all very beautifully done.' She expressed her distaste for 'the Low Church way of celebrating Holy Communion' because it so often seemed to her 'slovenly and unceremonious … the priest seeming to put his own personality into it instead of saying it in a level colourless way so that one gets the meaning without emphasis or the intrusion of personality.'[18] Nevertheless, some things were even too high for Macaulay, and she reported to Father Johnson that the most extreme church in London was St Magnus the Martyr's where the vicar, Father Clynes-Clinton, had relics, and could liquefy blood! She was glad that her Chapel attempted no such nonsense.

She became friendly with many priests in London, and engaged in correspondence with some of them, including a young priest named Gerard Irvine, whom she first met at a play at St Thomas's Regent Street – a church that she regarded as so extreme in its Anglo-Catholicism that 'it has, it seems, come full circle, and they *sit* at Mass, or so he says.'[19] Irvine took her out for drinks and sandwiches afterwards at a pub, and their friendship blossomed from there. Her faith also brought her other friends, such as Trevor Huddleston, whose anti-apartheid work she supported, Canon John Collins of St Paul's Cathedral, whose pacifism she shared, and the poet John Betjeman.

As she matured in faith, she came to appreciate going to a nonconformist church from time to time, especially The King's Weigh in London, receiving communion there because she fervently believed in intercommunion. In fact, she had a profoundly inclusive sense of Christianity. In an amusing account of a visit to a Butlins Holiday camp in 1955, which she described as 'rather like a visit to the moon, quite out of this world' and absurd for an adult but fun to be there with children (as she was), she reported the unexpected 'little camp church, Anglican, with a chaplain of great geniality to one and all.' As she reported to Father Johnson, 'A radio voice announced each morning at 7.29, "In one minute there will be a celebration of Holy Communion in the camp church". Disgusted and sleepy voice from the chalet on my left "What an entertainment".' She was impressed by the chaplain who 'welcomed everyone to Communion – Church, chapel, or whatever – though he was definitely Anglo-Catholic in his rites. That's the Christian spirit, surely. Imagine what our Lord would have said.'[20]

She developed a rule of life, going to Mass each morning, and then to church once or twice on Sundays, and making her confession regularly. But technology intervened then (as it does now). She came to question the wisdom of evening church because of the excellence of Sunday evening religious broadcasting – which she went to her club to watch, not having a television set herself. 'I quite see why religious people don't go to church as much as they did' she wrote to her sister in 1957, 'TV is so much more interesting and full of ideas. It is rather sad for the clergy, who naturally like a full church and a full collection.'[21]

At the heart of Macaulay's newly re-found faith was her conviction that she had 'always felt "Anglican" ... I mean, I have been an Anglo-agnostic; and even were I an atheist should be an Anglo-atheist.' And she reported a conversation with the poet Stephen Spender in 1952, who said to her that 'though he couldn't believe much of what Christianity taught and held, he was an Anglican, because he thought it such a good "framework for moral aspiration" so that the Church should be supported.' Even when she scarcely went to church, she said, except to look at the architecture or attend weddings, she was still an Anglican non-church-goer. It was, she said 'a matter of taste and affection'; but, more than that, 'it is in the blood and bones, at deeper levels than brain or will.' So, she continued, 'Perhaps it is a good thing, now that brain and will begin functioning again, to have that heritage to draw on. A kind of spiritual capital, laid up for one by one's ancestors and upbringing, and by various influences since. Certainly no merit of mine.' As she put it, 'What a heritage we have. I mean, we Anglicans. It is so incredibly beautiful.'[22] There are echoes here of Percy Dearmer, though I have found no reference to her having read his work; and her Anglo-Catholicism was not, primarily, of the English Use sort that Dearmer favoured.

This brings us to her 'frames' – not only that Anglicanism was 'a framework for good actions and aspirations' as the poet Stephen Spender said, but that we see God through frames, not directly, and those frames for Macaulay were decidedly Anglican. That is in part why this Anglican heritage was for her so important: the buildings, the music, the liturgy, were all ways in which she perceived God. The letters to Father

Johnson are full of discussions of hymns in *Hymns Ancient and Modern* and in Percy Dearmer's *English Hymnal*; churches she had gone to visit in the English countryside; as well as the history of liturgy – about which they were both very well informed – and much else. And the letters convey her own delight at being part of something bigger than oneself, in the Church; of belonging again: 'isn't it a wonderful corporate feeling of being carried along, being part of the body, not looking at it from outside, beyond a fence. And, as you say, everything in it fits gradually in, forming the pattern of the whole; and the bits one doesn't yet grasp, or that don't mean anything much to one, may one day. Anyhow, that doesn't matter to the whole pattern and movement in which one is involved, as if it was a great sweeping symphony that one can hear a little of the meaning now and then.'[23]

She also discussed with Father Johnson what she was reading, and much of it was from the English theological tradition, from Jeremy Taylor in the seventeenth century and William Law in the eighteenth century, to twentieth-century writers such as Gregory Dix on liturgy and Kenneth Kirk on moral theology. Father Johnson guided her, but she was also constantly browsing the theological and ecclesiastical shelves in the London Library. A few months into her new life of faith, she read Evelyn Underhill's 1921 book, *The Life of the Spirit and the Life of To-day* (from which I quoted in the Introduction). This is the book that Underhill wrote immediately after returning fully to the Church of England and perhaps that is why Macaulay found her point of view 'particularly sympathetic to me'.[24] It was a book she re-read several years later, as she found the chapter on psychology and the spirit 'v.g.' – 'I mean, exactly what I think myself, about the struggling up of man from his animal state, with all his animal desires still clinging to him.' She read Margaret Cropper's biography of Underhill when it came out in 1958, which she found interesting, not least because Underhill was 'very self-absorbed, and concerned with her spiritual state'.[25] She also reported to Father Johnson that she had met Underhill many years back 'who wasn't quite so good as her books'![26] Later (beginning in November 1955 and then annually until her death), she went on retreat to Pleshey. She asked Father Johnson, 'Do you know Pleshey Retreat House, I wonder? You may even have been there, I dare say. I was never there before. Evelyn Underhill used to take retreats there, I think. It is a nice place; I like its atmosphere. And the addresses couldn't have been better…'. She made notes of the addresses which were given by the Bishop of Tewksbury, Edward Henderson, whom she had got to know when he was Rector of St Paul's Knightsbridge and whose consecration she had attended earlier that year. She considered him 'an inspiring person.'[27] In her notes, she especially emphasized his point that conversion goes on, and the turning points in life are clear.[28] She had written to Father Johnson earlier that year, after hearing Father Henderson's Lent addresses: 'I am very much interested just now in "character" and how each moment and each thought builds it up.'[29]

Throughout the letters with Father Johnson, there is a sense of adventure in her new faith and the intellectual and spiritual exploration of it with a kindred spirit. They sent each other gifts, and Macaulay was hugely grateful, especially for the packages of books which Father Johnson thoughtfully sent to replenish her library: 'All those lovely books! Unpacking your parcels is like opening Chinese toys, one thing inside another – paper, stout envelope, soft packing, more paper (green, with elastic bands round it this time), and finally the book, always a lovely surprise.'[30] They had a shared interest in Latin grammar too, and loved, especially, to discuss the Latin of certain collects in their correspondence.

After about eighteen months of corresponding, they discovered that they were fourth cousins – they had the same great, great, great grandparents – and this was a huge delight to both of them, as they prized family relationships. Thereafter, Rose began to address Father Johnson as 'Dear Hamilton' or 'My dear Hamilton' rather than 'Father' noting, 'I certainly like to call you this, and I don't feel it interferes with or takes away from our relationship as it has been for so long. We are now relations in another sense, also, that is all.'[31]

The publication of the first volume, *Letters to a Friend*, in 1961, three years after Macaulay's death, caused controversy. It was still early in the 1960s, that decade having not quite yet become the radical sixties, and the discussion of a love affair with a married man in combination with the central theme of the book – Macaulay's return to the Church – made people question the ethics of making public such private letters. Reviews were mixed, and the newspapers' letters pages were full of opinions, for and against, the correspondence being published. The *Daily Mail* ran a headline: 'Did this priest betray this woman?' (12 October 1961). Father Johnson died just before the book came out, so he did not live to witness the controversy, but both the editor, Constance Babington Smith (Rose's cousin), and Rose's sister Jean, came in for some criticism. Jean had all along supported the publication of the letters, writing in 1960 to Babington Smith who was at that stage preparing the book:

> I look on them as a most moving story of the return, late in life, to the religion of her childhood of someone who had lost it for many years, as well as of penitence for a friendship which she felt to have been wrong. I think it may have a great influence for good on a generation which has largely lost its sense of faith and morals. Rose was so absolutely genuine, as well as highly intelligent, and capable of deep feeling. And everyone who knew her loved her. I know she would have wished above all things to be the means of helping others through their mistakes.[32]

Finally, some months after the book's publication, the Archbishop of Canterbury, Michael Ramsey, weighed in positively, writing to Constance Babington Smith of his support of the book: 'I find the letters immensely interesting, and I cannot but think that good will come of the book.' He added that he thought 'some very stupid things have been said in the controversy in some of the papers; it does not seem to me that there has been any impropriety in the publication of the letters.'[33]

The sense of Macaulay's gratitude for a second chance, which runs throughout the letters, is a testimony to faith. In 1952, Father Johnson had suggested to her that her novel

The World My Wilderness, published in 1950, the year their correspondence began, was largely an unconscious prayer. Macaulay replied to that suggestion as follows:

> Yes, I think you are right about my Wilderness being largely an unconscious prayer. Well, it got answered all right – more than one could have dreamed. Looking back, I can't think – I really *can't* think – how on earth I managed to get on for so long, turned away from it all, and not even realizing, except at moments, how much I needed it and wanted it. Blind and deaf and choked with the vanities of time, turning away from the 'riches of eternity.' Oh well. Of course I have missed a lot, from missing all those years; but I couldn't *value* it more than I do now that I have come to it at last.[34]

She was deeply grateful to Father Johnson:

> You have always met me halfway, or more than halfway, and one has the feeling that you really care. Then you understand all that I say or ask, with all its implications and overtones, and your answers always cover what I meant and add more to it; and I always understand what you mean. Incidentally, you also have a knack, which pleases me, of making me laugh a little even on a serious subject.[35]

And she also had a theology of gratitude for God's gifts and grace. Our own refusal to be hurried to faith does not tire out God's kindness for us, and God 'gives us these fresh chances, and lays these plans in "the exceeding riches of his grace in his kindness towards us".' It didn't necessarily make sense to her – 'All very odd. Why? That seems the enormous riddle of the human race and of God. Or, if not very odd, very overwhelming.'[36] Those around her remarked that she became gentler, nicer and Harold Nicholson, in his warm and positive review of the first volume of letters to Father Johnson, said of Macaulay, that after her (re)conversion, 'Her joyous faith halved her worries and doubled all her joys.'[37]

Some have suggested that the central character of Macaulay's last and most celebrated novel, *The Towers of Trebizond*, Laurie, a woman who has an affair with a married man, and also takes off on a strange trip to consider the viability of an Anglican mission to Turkey with her aunt Dot and the eccentric Anglo-Catholic priest Father Chantry-Pigg, was based on Macaulay herself, and that the novel was autobiographical, even though Laurie does not turn to the church at the end of the novel. And in the words of Aunt Dot to Laurie at the end of the novel, one may perhaps see Rose of immature faith in her youth and the Rose who returned to faith in her 70s. 'I think, my dear, the Church once used to be an opiate to you; a kind of euphoric drug. You dramatized it and yourself, you felt carried along in something aesthetically exciting and beautiful and romantic; you were a dilettante, escapist Anglican.' Rather, Aunt Dot continues: 'One mustn't lose sight of the hard core, which is, do this, do that, love your friends and like your neighbours, be just, be extravagantly generous, be honest, be tolerant, have courage, have compassion, use your wits and your imagination, understand the world you live in and be on terms with it, don't dramatize and dream of escape. Anyhow, that seems to be the

pattern, so far as we can make it out here. So come in again
when your eyes open, when you feel you can.'[38]

Macaulay did not deny the resonances, at least to Father
Johnson, to whom she wrote: 'I, too, felt Laurie's half-stunned
insensibility, and even aversion, towards the church, for some
time after the man I had loved for so long died. I don't take
Laurie far enough in her life to get to where she, as I did,
encounters some influence that brings her church-ward. But
of course it came: feeling as she always had about the Church
and about separation from God, she would not for very long
be outside it.'[39]

What both Macaulay and her character Laurie shared
most of all, perhaps, was their complexity. Macaulay believed
that people are interesting because they are a bundle of
contradictions. This made her own faith generous and open
because she had a sense of God as the one who had invited
her into a life of faith through the extraordinary ministry of a
kind, learned monk 3000 miles away.

Surely none of us can hear this generous theology of
second chances – third, fourth, fifth, sixth chances – enough.
Macaulay probably did not intend her letters to Father Johnson
to be published and, as we have seen, their publication caused
controversy. But they stand as a remarkable testimony to an
open, welcoming church, the God of surprises and second
chances, and the transformative power of forgiveness, as well
as the glories of Anglicanism, the infectious delight of an
intellectually and emotionally engaged faith, which interacts
with the world, and the significance of being part of something
much greater than ourselves.

Notes

1   *Letters to a Sister from Rose Macaulay*, ed. Constance Babington Smith (London: Collins, 1964), pp. 250 – 251

2   *Letters to a Friend from Rose Macaulay, 1950-1952*, ed. Constance Babington Smith (London: Collins, 1961), p. 29

3   Quoted in Constance Babington Smith, 'Introduction', *Letters to a Friend*, pp. 17 – 18

4   Jean Babington Macaulay to Constance Babington Smith, 3rd September, 1962, Emilie Rose Macaulay papers, Trinity College, Cambridge, ERM4/64.

5   *Letters to a Sister*, pp. 38, 76, 78

6   *Letters to a Sister*, p. 41

7   *Letters to a Friend*, p. 28

8   A.N. Wilson, 'Rose Macaulay' in *Founders and Followers: Literary Lectures given on the occasion of the 150th anniversary of the founding of The London Library* (London: Sinclair-Stevenson, 1992), p. 130

9   *Letters to a Friend*, p. 36

10 Conversation with Father David Allen, SSJE, May 31, 2017

11 Father Hamilton Johnson, SSJE, 'Our Conversation in Heaven.' Sermon preached in St. John's Church (Boston), Sunday morning, November 16, 1941 (Trinity xxiii), SSJE archives, Box 3.33, f.2

12 *Letters to a Friend*, p. 28

13 *Letters to a Friend*, p. 32

14 *Letters to a Friend*, p. 38

15 Father Hamilton Johnson, SSJE, Sermon on the Pharisee and the Publican, preached in S. John's Church, on August 16, 1942 (Trinity xi), SSJE archives, Box 3.33, f.2

16 *Letters to a Friend*, p. 39

17 *Letters to a Friend*, pp. 39, 48, 58, 59, 55

18 *Letters to a Sister*, p. 288

19 *Letters to a Friend*, pp. 155, 142

20 Rose Macaulay, *Last Letters to a friend 1952-1958*, ed. Constance Babington Smith (London: Collins, 1963), p. 210

21 *Letters to a Sister*, p. 246

22 *Letters to a Friend*, pp. 69, 257, 69, 110

23 *Letters to a Friend*, pp. 257

24 *Letters to a Friend*, p. 167

25 *Letters to a Sister*, pp. 196, 292

26 *Letters to a Friend*, p. 94

27 *Last Letters to a Friend*, pp. 210, 200, 192

28 'RM Notes of Retreat at Pleshey, conducted by Bp of Tewsbury, 1955', ERM 3/265, Trinity College, Cambridge, archives

29 *Last Letters to a Friend*, p. 195

30 *Letters to a Friend*, p. 177

31 *Letters to a Friend*, p. 287

32 Jean Babington Macaulay to Constance Babington Smith, 25 September 1960, ERM 4/32, Trinity College, Cambridge, archives

33 Archbishop Michael Ramsey to Constance Babington Smith, 24 October 1961, ERM 13/116, Trinity College, Cambridge, archives

34 *Letters to a Friend*, p. 292

35 *Letters to a Friend*, p. 88

36 *Letters to a Friend*, p. 71

37 Harold Nicholson, 'The joyous faith of Rose Macaulay,' *The Observer*, 22 October 1961

38 Rose Macaulay, *The Towers of Trebizond* (1956) (London: Collins, 1978), p. 220. For an example of this sort of interpretation of the novel, see David Hein, 'Rose Macaulay: A Voice from the Edge' in *C.S. Lewis and Friends: Faith and the Power of Imagination*, eds. David Hein and Edward Henderson (London: SPCK, 2011), pp. 93 – 115

39 *Last Letters to a Friend*, p. 233

Chapter 5

Spirituality and the Church today

'Church going has declined steadily and rapidly; this being a free and honest age, people no longer attend what they do not like.'

Percy Dearmer, 1919

'I think we may now say without exaggeration that the general modern judgment – not, of course, the clerical or orthodox judgment – is adverse to institutionalism; at least as it now exists.'

Evelyn Underhill, 1921

I began this book with these quotations from Percy Dearmer and Evelyn Underhill on the state of institutional religion and its distance from the personal spiritual quest of so many of their contemporaries a hundred years ago. Their words, repeated today, serve well as a pertinent commentary on our current situation.

The number of people ticking the 'none' box is increasing: in a 2016 British Social Attitudes (BSA) survey 53 per cent identified as 'none' – though, of course, as bishops reassure the faithful (and the media), 'none' does not necessarily translate to atheist. This was up from 48 per cent in 2015, according to BSA figures, and has gradually increased from 31% in 1983 when the BSA survey began.[1] In the USA, in a wide-ranging piece of research on America's changing religious landscape, run by the Pew Research Center in 2014, the number of 'nones' was calculated at 23 per cent, up – very rapidly – from 16% in 2007; this figure rises to 35 per cent 'nones' in 2014 amongst those dubbed millennials (those born between 1981 and 1996).[2]

The 1960s is usually regarded as the decade when this religious decline, or what we might call a 'splitting out' from the church, began. In terms of numbers, that may indeed be the case. But I hope that the preceding chapters - with their portraits of Anglicans who had complex spiritual and religious lives, not always at the heart of the church, often on the margins – have shown that the split between institutional religion and spirituality is a phenomenon with which people have grappled throughout the twentieth century. It is the wisdom and experience of these early to mid-twentieth-century Anglicans that I seek to bring to bear on our twenty-first-century musing on this dilemma.

Underhill, Dearmer and Macaulay all had a deep understanding – and in the cases of Underhill and Macaulay a profound experiential knowledge – that to absent oneself from Church is not to be without a spiritual thirst or longing for a structure in which to ask ultimate questions. Cultural commentators have continued to remark on this dilemma throughout the twentieth century, and into the twenty-first. Three years after the writer Stephen Spender was remarking to Rose Macaulay that he thought the Church of England a good 'framework for moral aspiration', Philip Larkin wrote his poem 'Church Going' (1955) in which he expresses this tension between church decline and a longing for a proper 'seriousness.' The narrator of the poem wonders 'When churches fall completely out of use/What we shall turn them into'. And then he expresses the insight that there will always be seekers, visitors to the ancient sites of wisdom, because of what those abandoned churches represented: 'someone will forever be surprising/A hunger in himself to be more serious/And gravitating with it to this ground /Which he once heard was proper to grow wise in.'

We live in the midst of all kinds of spiritual activity, representing a thirst for seriousness and a desire to make better sense of our time – both our daily routine and our lifespan: meditation, yoga, mindfulness, and endless apps for all of those things. Activities that are apparently secular take on spiritual tropes: think of the exercise group 'Soul Cycle' - not only its name, but its candle-lit atmosphere, its guru exercise leaders, its branding slogans such as 'find your soul' and, even, its early selling of front-row cycles to those who sign up as special members (reminiscent of the buying of pews in previous centuries).

'What a heritage we have!' said Rose Macaulay, but the Church is not always good at harnessing and using that heritage to engage with the seekers who are meditating and cycling their way to 'meaning'. Macaulay meant the Anglican heritage of literature, music, art, architecture, but the entire heritage of Christianity is one in which a proper 'seriousness' can be explored. The current focus on increasing discipleship in the Church of England is sometimes successful, but it can be both narrow and - despite the fact that it is all about meeting people 'where they are' - rather churchy in its perspective. Likewise the American Episcopal Church's current focus on being the Episcopal branch of the Jesus movement can be appealing, with its traditional revival-style events, its clear articulation of the Episcopal Church's identity and renewed focus on justice; but it is still largely focused on those who already belong. In other words, the prevalent approach of the churches is mostly about getting people into the pews on Sundays, and the mission strategies often miss the mark – even for that goal. So maybe there is something wrong with both the goal and the strategy?

Most people do not (at least initially) see any point in going to church, so trying to get them to do that is not necessarily an effective form of engagement. Why go to church (or, indeed, engage in any form of corporate worship) is an obvious question, as Percy Dearmer realized a hundred years ago. Mindfulness can be practised while washing the dishes; meditation can be done alone. A meaningful spiritual life can be practised solo, and all the damaging nonsense of the churches can be avoided. This is the – understandable –

attitude of many people today. In my experience, churches do not grow just by inviting people to come to worship services. What if we really tapped into our heritage to offer what we know people are looking for? – beauty, justice, ways of organizing our over-committed lives, a relationship with something beyond us, seriousness about existential questions, and joyous community that can support us in our brokenness and give us hope. Casper Ter Kuile and Angie Thurston, Ministry Innovation Fellows at Harvard Divinity School, in their research on alternative communities that attract millennials and function rather like religion, emphasize six recurring themes: community, personal transformation, social transformation, purpose-finding, creativity, and accountability.[3] We have all that and more in Christianity, and we have it in abundance in the Anglican tradition: both Percy Dearmer and Rose Macaulay knew that, and celebrated it.

We need *pathways* into that heritage for those who do not know it. Such pathways will not always result in more people at church on a Sunday, and we would do well not to make that our expected outcome. But they may well result in transformed lives - which is what faith, in the end, is about.

Beauty, community and justice

People respond to beauty. We are drawn to that which is beautiful because it feeds our souls. My experience of having been dean of a cathedral suggests that the arts are a major pathway into the exploration of spirituality for those who are on the edges of organized religion and seeking meaning. We founded a resident artist program at Grace Cathedral in San Francisco soon after I arrived as dean, and through that program brought drama, the visual arts, music and even cookery to the cathedral. This opened the doors to those who did not normally 'do religion' and made it clear that the cathedral was for the whole city, not just the religious. These programs attracted those from around the city who were interested in exploring something beyond themselves, many of whom began to be interested in what we were doing the rest of the time – not least, worship. One consequence was that the congregation grew by 15 per cent in four years. Another was that many people felt newly comfortable in entering a church. Yet another was a realization amongst regular churchgoers that the arts are always directing our attention to the divine, and can open our eyes anew, again and again, to the glory of God, *and* to the experiences of those beyond ourselves.

Our Anglican heritage is full of beauty, as Rose Macaulay so often articulated to Father Johnson, much of it these days neglected. We would be wise to remember people's love for the beauty of their parish churches (especially – but not always – medieval, in the British context); beautiful buildings that are often neglected in these days of efficiency and number crunching. Church administrators and bureaucrats are good at providing empirical evidence as to why certain (especially rural) churches should be closed for lack of attendance at services, and overworked vicars can give reasons for paying no attention to the fabric of a little-attended church, but this ignores the element of aesthetics and the wider community, making the reasons for a church's existence narrowly 'churchy'.

In fact, people who do not attend church often have an attachment to the local church for its beauty and for its potential to gather people. How then do we harness people's attachment to their local churches – or, at least, appreciation of their churches' beauty - and play to the church's strengths? How do we encourage and enable the people of a parish or community – churched and unchurched - to take responsibility for the upkeep of some of the most beautiful church buildings, which are often sorely neglected by a cash-strapped central church administration? How might the ideals of aesthetics and community-making be joined here? Might parish churches that would otherwise be neglected (remember Larkin's poem) become centres for the community and community-building, used every day of the week for yoga, book clubs, concerts, senior citizen lunches and much more?

Other churches might become permanently multi-use in order to serve the community, like St James in West Hampstead, London, a Victorian Gothic church, the interior of which was transformed by the congregation under the creative leadership of its most recent vicar, Andrew Foreshew-Cain, to host not only a worshipping space but also the local Post Office, a café and stationery shop, and a large and popular children's play area, all of which the parish owns and operates. The idea of 'Church' that lies behind this space is clearly articulated on St James's website: 'Fundamental to our faith is the belief that we are all welcomed by God. The Church is not a club but a community of those whom God has welcomed and that welcome is for each of us.' This theology of the Church therefore influences how the congregation members think about both their interaction with the wider community and the use of their own church resources: 'Because this is our community it is important that we play a part in the life of the area and we do try to get involved with local groups and organisations as well as provide services and events ourselves. We are aware that we are blessed with the resources of buildings and people and we use them in the service of others because we believe that we see God in our service of others.' As the parish website notes, this makes the church 'a bustling centre of community and full of people all day every day. This makes us unique among the Churches in the country (yes, country) and we are very proud of what has been achieved and offered. Nonetheless St James is still a living Church and that atmosphere is tangible to all who come for the first time, whether to worship, simply light a candle or just to post a letter. Come and see for yourself.'

The point of this expansion of St James's activities is not necessarily to get more people in on a Sunday for services, but to serve the community and witness to God's love. The congregation members do this with a clear sense of God's justice, stating 'We quite deliberately set out to be welcoming to all people, regardless of gender, sexuality, age, race, physical ability or mental health.' And they fully supported their vicar when he came into conflict with the episcopal authorities for his marriage to a man. They are also clear that everything they do is founded in their Christian beliefs, and grounded in common worship and prayer: 'We are Christians and we pray and worship, it is the lifeblood of our lives. So we take prayer and worship seriously as the foundations of everything we do.' This worship is done with a serious attention to aesthetics, and excellent music. [4]

Beauty is connected to both justice and community precisely because it puts us in touch with something that is beyond us. It puts *us* into perspective, reminding us that we are not at the centre of the universe. This is what the twentieth-century French philosopher and theologian Simone Weil said: that beauty requires us to give up our imaginary position as the centre. The novelist Iris Murdoch called this 'unselfing'. While Weil had a complex relationship to faith, and Murdoch was an atheist, they were both articulating something that is central to a life of faith, and the transformation that faith can bring when we realize life is 'not all about me'. The Episcopal priest Paul Fromberg writes 'Beauty is costly; it calls us to see the world in new ways, ways that are tempered by the beauty we behold. We cannot unsee beauty that has been deeply seen. This is one of the reasons that beauty has the power to transform us.'[5]

Beauty in worship can therefore draw us into the life of faith. This is one of the reasons that cathedrals are growing when some other segments of the Church are not. The number of people attending services at Anglican cathedrals in England went up by 30 per cent in the first decade of the twenty-first century, representing a rise in attendees at worship services of about 3 percent a year. Cathedrals evoke beauty and mystery through their architecture, liturgy, music and art.

Of course, this sense of beauty and mystery is not, and need not be, confined to cathedrals. Percy Dearmer's intention, in his *Parson's Handbook*, was to give parish priests a set of principles and tools to make both their churches and their liturgies beautiful. If his church, St Mary's, Primrose Hill, was the iconic church for liturgy and beauty in the early twentieth century, then St Gregory of Nyssa, an Episcopal Church in San Francisco, would have a strong claim to hold that status for the early twenty-first century. Two Episcopal priests, who had been students together on the East coast and wanted to form a church where the liturgy would form the community, founded St Gregory of Nyssa in 1978. Incorporated into the worship are elements from a variety of traditions, including Eastern Orthodox prayers and music, the silence of the Society of Friends, Shaker hymns and dance, and much more. The purpose-built church has a sequence of glorious icons of dancing saints – ranging from Teresa of Avila and Francis of Assisi to Archbishop Desmond Tutu and the anthropologist Margaret Mead - which circle the rotunda, with Christ in glory in their midst. The music is sung *a capella*, usually in four parts, led by a choir.

Its current rector, Paul Fromberg, writes, not unlike Dearmer: 'God's revelation brings beauty. This is more than a claim about the meaning of beauty, more than an aesthetic hope. The encounter with beauty is not only a gift *from* God, it is an experience *of* God. Beauty is the glory of God, not only a way that we talk of God's glory.' And, like Dearmer, Fromberg offers a sacramental view of beauty: 'When we look for God, we don't receive a clear picture as much as a luminous darkness. God's shape is a mystery, always approaching us. Beauty is how God chooses to be known.'[6]

Fromberg develops his theology of beauty to show the ways in which it shapes how we think about human nature and therefore how we interact with one another. 'God uses beauty to reveal the truth of our identity. God's beauty stirs within our hearts and minds, transforming us into beauty. It is God's will that we become beautiful, just as God is beautiful. This is our natural state: we are God's creatures, made in God's image, destined for beauty.[7] It is no surprise, then, that St Gregory's links beauty, worship and justice in the way it *does* church. Just as Dearmer advocated that all people become involved in making church and making art together, so the people of St Gregory's - strangers and friends alike - make music, worship and art as a community. Fromberg writes: 'Art is normal for us. It isn't something that only a select group gets to make; everyone can offer their work to reveal the beauty of God in the community.'[8]

St Gregory's also runs a food pantry for those who need fresh produce and groceries, and this food is *intentionally* served from around the altar – not from a separate basement or parish hall. Here, there is no difference between being spiritually fed and physically fed. Here, liturgy shapes social practice. Here, the food pantry is run by those who came – and still come – to receive the food they need. And beauty is important: when you walk into the food pantry, it looks like a glorious farmers' market. A key inspiration for the food pantry for its founder Sara Miles (Fromberg's partner in ministry for many years) was the set of two engravings on the purpose-built altar. The first, from Luke's Gospel, is an insult to Jesus: 'This guy welcomes sinners and eats with them.' The second is taken from the seventh-century Isaac of Nineveh: 'Did not our Lord share his table with tax collectors and harlots? So do not distinguish between worthy and unworthy. All must be equal for you to love and serve.'[9] Beauty, community and justice are all intentionally intertwined at St Gregory Nyssa, San Francisco, as they are at St James, West Hampstead.

What, then, if we make aesthetics a primary criterion for what we do in church, rather than a secondary consideration? What would happen if we took beauty as seriously as we take other factors in the use and preservation of our church buildings and our worship? How might beauty de-centre us in exactly the ways that Christianity urges us - to focus our lives not on self, but on love of God and love of neighbour, naturally leading us to issues of justice and the creation of community. To put beauty first in all these cases would be, as Percy Dearmer put it, returning to first principles. How about we return to first principles?

Prayer and Time

Being drawn into the life of our Christian heritage is one thing, knowing what to do when you get there is another. I have long been struck by the ways in which we Christians are not so good at teaching people how to *practise* faith, by which I mean, prayer and contemplation, and the work in the world - love of neighbour, and commitment to community and justice - that flows from that foundation of prayer and adopting a rule of life. It is easy to find out how to meditate: you can go to a Buddhist centre in almost any town and go to a weekly or even daily class that will teach you the techniques of meditation, or you can find numerous 'how-to' apps. Similarly, you can find any number of books, apps and classes on mindfulness. But if you want to learn, in a very practical way, how to pray in the Christian tradition, it is not so easy. Entering a church service, with its multiple pieces of paper, books and instructions can be bewildering, and it is unlikely that you will find a weekday evening class on how to pray. And yet Christianity has a wonderfully rich heritage of contemplation, meditation and prayer.

Evelyn Underhill was committed to teaching people how to pray, and believed that anyone could do it. She did this through her writings, her spiritual direction, and the leading and promotion of retreats. Those of us in the churches will need to continue to find creative ways of introducing people who are curious but uninformed, questing but disengaged, to the spiritual heritage of our tradition. Retreats continue to be important for the spiritually curious. The monks of the Society of St John the Evangelist, Father Johnson's order, are acutely aware that those who come on retreat to their monastery and Guesthouse are changing in demographic – often younger, but not necessarily of any particular faith. The SSJE website notes that the monks 'aim to offer spaces of silence, beauty, and simple comfort to guests, for an hour, a day, or for a longer visit.' In the website's Q and A section, after the question 'Why might I want to go on retreat?' God-language does not enter the answer until a couple of sentences in:

> Taking a time away from the demands of everyday life, to be quiet, to pray, to worship, to read, rest, and relax, allows us to refocus our lives on what is most important to us. Some people come on retreat at moments of transition, where they feel the need for particular discernment. Others come on retreat simply to refresh and renew their spirit. Our relationship with God, like all human relationships,

113

needs attention and care to grow. Times of retreat allow us to turn our whole selves to God, to listen and be attentive to the voice of God. Many people experience retreats as times when God seems particularly near.[10]

The language is deliberately aimed at both the seeker and the believer, and all those at the many points in between.

Take, too, the example of The British Pilgrimage Trust, which organizes pilgrimages across traditional routes in Britain, but aims 'to renew the tradition according to modern needs, to create an open spiritual activity without religious prescription.'[11] It also offers the option to stay in churches, overnight, thereby creating another revenue stream for beautiful parish churches. As Janet Gough, director of the Church of England's cathedral and church buildings division, comments: 'Churches are experimenting with offering places for pilgrims to stay. It is a great way to use the buildings and the donations can help support the church community, as well as the building's fabric and long-term care.'[12]

The wisdom of the early twentieth-century figures we have considered in this book, and these renewed traditions for and of our own day, remind us that to engage in this kind of attention to God we need to be intentional about ordering and re-ordering our time. Indeed, re-ordering our time makes us better stewards of it, with the theological understanding of time as a gift from God - to be used wisely and with gratitude, as Geoffrey Tristram SSJE reminds us. 'Time is not an endless succession of things to do, bitter sighs, tired nights, and disappointments ... Each new day will never come again, which makes it incredibly precious.'[13]

Reginald Somerset Ward taught that to live with intention we need a rule of life. We might say that we need such a rule of life now more than ever, as technology increasingly intrudes into our lives. The amount of personal leisure time we each have has rapidly decreased, as we give more and more of it over to technological activities. Ward's urging to create a rule of life may therefore be especially important for us in these technologically dogged days. When I gave my Sarum Lecture on Reginald Somerset Ward in Salisbury the Dean, June Osborne, said, 'Oh, we need a discipline of our devices.' It is a wonderful phrase.

We do not get to change our habits around time unless we consciously prepare to do so, and then undertake to stick by our new framework or rule of life. Because – remember! – those in the tech business have a vested interest in keeping us hooked. Everything about the internet and social media is about getting you to click on to the next thing and stay on the web for as long as possible because that is the business model. We need to be on the web to read the ads; we need to be on the web for big data to be created; and we need to be on the web for our browsing to be analysed, so that marketing can be targeted at us.[14] This means that we have to be intentional about creating a discipline of our devices.

Making such time and sticking to our rule of life is therefore not easy, and even monks admit that. Geoffrey Tristram SSJE writes:

> Even in the Monastery, it is difficult for us to keep to the use of time that our Rule prescribes. We Brothers are as prone as anyone to overwork, to misuse time. It's

115

a constant problem. And when the Chapel bell rings, making us stop our work by calling us to the Divine Office, it can sometimes be rather annoying! It sounds out across the Monastery and forces us to stop what we are doing – probably right when we are in the thick of it – and we sigh a little, because what we were doing just then was no doubt something that seemed quite important. But the bell reminds us that we're not here just to work, just to do and to accomplish. We're here to glorify God by our lives. The bell, which makes us stop, actually calls us back to our truest identity.[15]

We each need the equivalent of the monastic bell in our lives – calling us to a practice that helps us first to know, and then repeatedly return to, our truest identity. And Reginald Somerset Ward's injunction to put prayer, recreation and work in that order challenges us to ask and determine what our priorities are.

Conclusion

Evelyn Underhill wrote that the education of the mystical self lies in self-simplification, and she knew that stepping into that quieter and simpler way of being allowed the rebirth of the self. Reginald Somerset Ward urges us to take that step: to embrace the adventure of knowing ourselves and God, learning about the spiritual life by daily experiments. Percy Dearmer encourages us to take a further step: to appreciate the beauty of liturgy and corporate worship, and from that place to engage in the work of justice. Rose Macaulay lived with a deep knowledge of the glories of our Christian heritage and – most importantly – her life and her conversations with a gentle, kind monk are testimony to the second chances that await us all.

Notes

1 http://www.natcen.ac.uk/news-media/press-releases/2017/september/british-social-attitudes-record-number-of-brits-with-no-religion/

2 'America's Changing Religious Landscape,' Pew Research Forum, 2015 – see http://www.pewforum.org/2015/05/12/americas-changing-religious-landscape/

3 See their report, *How We Gather* at https://caspertk.files.wordpress.com/2015/04/how-we-gather.pdf

4 For all these statements about the purpose and mission of St James, West Hampstead, see the website of the church: http://www.churchnw6.co.uk/

5 Paul Fromberg, *The Art of Transformation: Three Things the Churches Do That Change Everything* (New York: Church Publishing, 2017) pp. 15, 24

6 Fromberg, *The Art of Transformation,* pp. 20, 18. Fromberg acknowledges his debt to Hans Urs von Balthasar's theology of beauty.

7 Fromberg, *The Art of Transformation,* p. 18

8 Fromberg, *The Art of Transformation,* p. 22

9 See Sara Miles, *Take This Bread: A Radical Conversion* (New York: Ballantine Books, 2007)

10 See the SSJE website: ssje.org

11 See their website: Britishpilgrimage.org

12 Quoted in 'Churches offer B&B (Bed and Bible)'in *The Times*, April 30, 2016

13 Br. Geoffrey Tristram, *Time: Redeeming the Gift* (Cambridge, MA: SSJE, no date), p. 8

14 See Adam Alter, *Irresistible: The Rise of Addictive Technology and the Business of Keeping Us Hooked* (New York: Penguin Press, 2017)

15 Tristram, *Time,* p. 5

Select Bibliography

Selected articles and books that may be most useful for further readings are given here. Some are not in print, but can be acquired secondhand.

1. Evelyn Underhill

The Letters of Evelyn Underhill, ed. Charles Williams (London: Longmans, Green and Co., 1943) – with several subsequent editions

The Making of a Mystic: New and Selected Letters of Evelyn Underhill, ed. Carol Poston (Urbana and Chicago: The University of Illinois Press, 2010)

Evelyn Underhill, *Mysticism: A Study in the Nature and Development of Man's Spiritual Consciousness* (London: Methuen, 2011) – republished in many subsequent editions

Evelyn Underhill, *Practical Mysticism* (1914) (New York: Dover Books, 2000)

Evelyn Underhill, *The Life of the Spirit and the Life of Today* (New York: E.P. Dutton, 1922)

Collected Papers of Evelyn Underhill, ed. Lucy Menzies (London: Longmans, Green and Co., 1946)

Christopher Armstrong, *Evelyn Underhill 1875 - 1941: An Introduction to her Life and Writings* (London: Mowbrays, 1975)

Annice Callahan, *Evelyn Underhill: Spirituality for Daily Living* (Lanham, MD: University Press of America, 1997)

Margaret Cropper, *The Life of Evelyn Underhill. An Intimate Portrait of the Groundbreaking Author of* Mysticism (1958) (Woodstock, VT: Skylight Paths Publishing, 2003)

Dana Greene, *Evelyn Underhill. Artist of the Infinite Life* (New York: Crossroad Publishing, 1990)

Jane Shaw, 'Varieties of Mysticism in William James and other Moderns', History of European Ideas (Vol. 43, Issue 3, 2017), pp. 226 – 240

2. Reginald Somerset Ward and 'The Road'

Reginald Somerset Ward's books are hard to acquire except for *To Jerusalem*, which has been reprinted in recent years. I therefore recommend Edmund Morgan's book, easy to buy second hand, as that contains extracts from many of his writings.

Reginald Somerset Ward, *To Jerusalem: Devotional Studies in Mystical Religion* (London: The S. Christopher Press, 1931) – republished in 1994 by Continuum, with an introduction by Susan Howatch

Reginald Somerset Ward, *The Way: devotional studies in mystical religion* (London: Church of England Sunday School Institute, 1922)

John Habgood, 'Waiting for God', the Twelfth Eric Symes Abbott lecture (London, The Dean's Office, King's College, London, 1997). This can be downloaded from the internet at: https://www.kcl.ac.uk/aboutkings/principal/dean/thedean/12th%20ESA%20lecture%201997.pdf

Edmund R. Morgan, ed., *Reginald Somerset Ward 1881 – 1962. His Life and Letters* (London: A. R. Mowbray and Co., 1963)

3. Percy Dearmer and his circle

Percy Dearmer, *The Parson's Handbook* (London: Grant Richards, 1899) – multiple subsequent editions published by Oxford University Press

Percy Dearmer, *The Art of Public Worship* (London and Oxford: A.R. Mowbray and Co., 1919)

Percy Dearmer, *Art and Religion* (London: SCM Press, 1924)

Nan Dearmer, *The Life of Percy Dearmer* (London: The Book Club, 1941)
Donald Gray, *Percy Dearmer: A Parson's Pilgrimage* (Norwich: Canterbury Press, 2000)

Frances Knight, *Victorian Christianity at the Fin-de-Siecle: The Culture of English Religion in a Decadent Age* (London: I. B. Tauris, 2016), chapter 9

Alison Falby, 'Maude Royden's Guildhouse: A Nexus of Religious Change in Britain between the Wars' in *Historical Papers 2004: Canadian Society of Church History*

Sheila Fletcher, *Maude Royden, A Life* (Oxford: Basil Blackwell, 1989)

4. Rose Macaulay

Rose Macaulay, *Letters to a Sister from Rose Macaulay*, ed. Constance Babington Smith (London: Collins, 1964)

Rose Macaulay, *Letters to a Friend from Rose Macaulay, 1950-1952*, ed. Constance Babington Smith (London: Collins, 1961)

Rose Macaulay, *Last Letters to a friend 1952 -1958* ed. Constance Babington Smith (London: Collins, 1963)

Rose Macaulay, *The Towers of Trebizond* (1956) - numerous reprints since

Constance Babbington-Smith, *Rose Macaulay* (London: Collins, 1972)

Sarah LeFanu, *Rose Macaulay: A Biography* (London: Virago, 2003)

David Hein, 'Rose Macaulay: A Voice from the Edge' in *C.S. Lewis and Friends: Faith and the Power of Imagination*, David Hein and Edward Henderson (London: SPCK, 2011)

INDEX

INDEX